Service Excellence
@
Novell

Service Excellence
@
Novell

Taking Customer Service from Cost to Profit

Nova Vista Publishing's Best Practices Editors

Available from Nova Vista Publishing:
<u>Business Books</u>
Win-Win Selling
Vendre gagnant-gagnant (French edition of Win-Win Selling)
Versatile Selling
S'adapter pour mieux vendre (French edition of Versatile Selling)
Socal Styles Handbook
I Just Love My Job!
Leading Innovation
Time Out for Leaders
Grown-Up Leadership
Service Excellence @ Novell
<u>Nature Books</u>
Return of the Wolf

How to order: single copies may be ordered online at www.novavistapub.com or from book shops and online retailers.

ISBN 90-77256-11-3   D/2006/9797/2
Printed in Singapore
20 19 18 17 16 15 14 13 12 11 10 9 8 7 6 5 4 3 2
Cover design: Astrid De Deyne
Text design: Softwin, Tiny Adriaensen
Editorial development: Andrew Karre

Contents

Foreword 7

Introduction – Transforming Customer Service 9

1. Setting the Stage 17

2. Picking a Partner 29

3. Training Skeptics and Supporters 41

4. Learning Key Concepts 55

5. Integrating: Expansion, Reinforcement, and Measurement 85

6. Lessons Learned 103

Index 108

About the Authors 111

FOREWORD

"Customer support is the toughest job in business," remarked Marion Bunch when we began discussing this book. People who do it must perform consistently in top form, despite the sometimes challenging emotional conditions customers bring to each contact. Why? Because at that moment of contact, customer support people *are* the company,

That is why service excellence can make a huge difference in any organization's odds of success. Novell's transformation of customer support shows how delivering service excellence can change what is often a cost center into a source of profit and growth for the company, as well as a source of personal satisfaction for the people involved. So that's why we wrote this book.

If you are an executive or business owner, you'll be interested in it as a model for making sustainable change on any front in an organization. For you, the customer support angle may be an example that stands in for another business problem you are concerned with today. The message for you lies in the top-down, comprehensive process that Novell used.

If you are a manager of customer support people, you will find insights about how critical managing, modeling, coaching, and measuring the new skills are in a successful transformation.

If you are on the front line of support, you will probably identify with many of the people quoted. And you'll appreciate the chapter on the techniques and tools that Novell's technical support engineers and their managers have learned to use with such remarkable success. While it doesn't have the same impact as live practice, there is plenty here that will help you do your job better, give your customers greater satisfaction, and also give you greater personal fulfillment in your work.

We would like to thank all the folks at Novell and Wilson Learning for their generous input in this book: Cory Bench, Marion Bunch, Lynn Collins, Marc Cordes, Dave Cutler, Sukanta Dash, Gemma de Koning, Rodrigo Gomez, Barry Haug, Harsh Jaitly, Lorin Jensen, Wouter Kampshoff, Dennis Lauw, Michael Leimbach, Bruce Lowry,

Mike Lyons, Carl Palme, Brad Palmer, Derek Paxton, Tevilla Riddell, Winfried Schwarzer, Chad Smith-Knott, Jim Sumsion, Akos Szechy, David Yesford, and Igor Zotkin.

All in all, we hope that while this is a quick-reading book, it will leave you with a lot to think about and act on in your own organization. We wish you all the best in that endeavor.

The Nova Vista Publishing Best Practices Editors

INTRODUCTION

TRANSFORMING CUSTOMER SERVICE

TRANSFORMING CUSTOMER SERVICE

This book tells the story of a remarkably successful change at Novell, Inc. As you read on, you will see how Novell's commitment to a particular problem-solving approach allowed it to transform its customer service group, Novell Technical Services, from a cost center into a significant profit center worldwide. Moreover, it enabled Novell to attract and retain more customers by giving them highly valuable, satisfying, personalized service, while giving the customer support employees more fulfillment in their own work.

Unlike Microsoft, a giant competitor, Novell helps customers knit together their existing information technology systems and infrastructure, integrating open (non-proprietary) and proprietary software in enterprise-wide solutions, all around the world.

To play in this arena, a company simply must have excellent technical know-how. In the last few years, it has virtually become a commodity. Fortunately for Novell, its reputation in this area is excellent. Providing support costs a lot, and providing excellent support costs even more. So Novell's leadership faced some interesting challenges: how to make Novell uniquely attractive to customers and deliver value so superb that customers would pay for support. A new strategy was called for.

The strategy would need to address Novell's external business drivers (competition, technical know-how evolving into a commodity) and internal business drivers (growing the customer base, moving support from cost to revenue).

Three strategies for change

Knowing the technical excellence was in place, but recognizing it was soon to become a commodity, Novell's technical services leaders determined how they wanted to transform Novell's customer service to make it a source of competitive advantage. They identified three key strategies:

- Provide more value.
- Make service personalized.
- Customize it to the customer's business needs.

However, the simplicity of these goals belies the challenge of making it happen. The model and the people both had to change, fundamentally.

Novell selected Wilson Learning Corporation to partner with its customer support group to make this change. Before we begin the Novell story itself, let's take a brief look at the general premises that Wilson Learning uses in its work with clients. The approach is called Human Performance Improvement (HPI).

HPI basics

HPI takes a holistic approach to change in organizations. It recognizes that when each person in an organization can say how his or her work supports the organization's key strategies, when the person has the skills and tools to perform successfully, and when management can support and coach these skills, the strategies are much more likely to produce their intended results. Furthermore, when employees know they play a part in supporting key strategies, they gain a feeling of fulfillment, allowing them to perform at their best every day. They recognize that strategy execution is everyone's job, which is a very strongly empowering idea.

Leaders must therefore be able to persuasively articulate their key strategies and define how each unit and person needs to perform to support them. They need to engage employees in the vision.

THE HUMAN PERFORMANCE IMPROVEMENT MODEL

What is most significant about the HPI approach is that it is comprehensive and holistic. All the elements represented schematically here are actually very dynamic, interactive factors in making a successful, sustainable transformation of any kind in an organization.

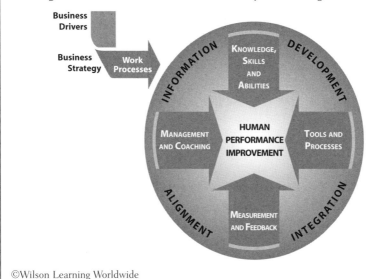

©Wilson Learning Worldwide

If the people carrying out strategy day by day lack the skills or tools needed to succeed, leaders must invest in their development. This may mean training, process improvement, performance measurement changes, new equipment, different policies – a whole raft of things could be involved. But although common sense tells us that you need to define the problem before you set out to solve it, too often a new slogan, costly sales conference, or training event gets launched, *and nothing changes*. The problem isn't properly defined, so the chances are good that these actions will not have the effect intended.

Clearly, if the organization does not take a comprehensive view of the problem and fixes only part of it successfully, the odds of overall success are threatened.

The HPI approach asks leaders to be able to answer a rather daunting list of questions like these:

1. Can you state your business strategy in a compelling way? What is it?
2. Do employees understand how their work supports that strategy?
3. What problems are preventing you from executing your strategy successfully?
4. What data do you have that helps define the problems?
5. What is missing now – what is the gap between your current situation and your desired one?
6. What does management need in order to lead comprehensive, sustainable change? How can you provide it?
7. What skills and knowledge would help employees support strategy better? How can you prepare them better?
8. How can you ensure that the new skills and knowledge are reinforced and embedded, for both managers and employees?
9. What work processes or structures are working contrary to your strategy, and how should they be changed to support it?
10. How will you know when you have made a successful change? What measurement tools do you need?

In their work with clients, Wilson Learning consultants first consider the business drivers, internal and external; the business strategy; and the existing business processes, which set the stage for action. To work out a solution using the HPI approach, the consultants group questions and activities into four clusters that occur in support of a business strategy. These clusters focus on Information, Development, Integration and Alignment.

EXTERNAL AND INTERNAL BUSINESS DRIVERS AND STRATEGY

As we have seen, Novell had a good notion of its external and internal business drivers and a clearly articulated strategy. This enabled Novell to make clear what its current situation was when it partnered with

Wilson Learning to develop the solution. Let's look now at the remaining clusters that complete the HPI model, in general terms, so you can see how the particulars fill in throughout the rest of this book.

INFORMATION

This cluster addresses questions related to performance issues, like these:

- How does performance affect the execution of our strategy in our organization?
- What business processes are affected?
- What are the sources of the performance problem?
- How are work processes affected? What skills and tools are required?

The outcome of work in this phase gives leaders a clear understanding of the performance standards required to successfully execute the strategy and achieve the performance goals.

DEVELOPMENT

This phase addresses the question, "How can we best address the performance gaps that keep us from executing strategy?" You might think the answer is simple: training and skill development. But while learning new skills is often part of the Development answer, rarely is it skill development alone. Therefore, it is important in the Development phase to identify the skill gaps, work process gaps, tool gaps, management support gaps, and measurement gaps that all contribute to the performance gap. The outcome provides a road map for change.

INTEGRATION

This phase of activity asks, "How do we insure that the new skills are used?" We all know that if you take people out of their normal environment, teach them new skills, then put them back into the same old environment, it does not take long for them to revert to former ways of working. So this phase addresses how to integrate the new learning, tools, systems, and approaches inside the current systems and ways that people work. Integration does not suggest that everything needs to change, though it may include enhancing technology, changing work processes, providing job aids, and changing how performance is measured and rewarded. The key idea is to maintain what worked and improve on that by integrating these solutions so they get embedded through a long-term approach.

ALIGNMENT

This activity cluster addresses the larger picture. It asks, "How do we insure that all key stakeholders support the improvement effort?" A key executive, or even an individual manager, can easily derail a change initiative. The Alignment phase identifies the actions that an organization's leadership needs to take to keep everyone pulling in the same direction:

- What executive messages will compel others to change their behaviors?
- What do individual managers need to do to support and coach their employees?
- What do owners, stockholders, and customers need to know so they support the strategy?

If the leadership of an organization can get these questions answered and acted on, genuine transformation has a good chance of flourishing.

While the sequence and content of these clusters and the activity needed to address these questions will vary from organization to organization, Wilson Learning has found that when organizations systematically focus on these elements of Human Performance Improvement, they increase the likelihood of successful change and improved strategy execution dramatically.

Now let's get into the story of how these elements unfolded as Novell transformed its customer support services.

CHAPTER ONE

SETTING THE STAGE

CHAPTER ONE

SETTING THE STAGE

This story is all about people: their dedication to helping Novell serve its customers so they can fulfill their visions – and so Novell can fulfill its own. The main players are Novell employees and the Human Performance Improvement consultants who worked with them to effect a comprehensive transformation of the way customer service is perceived and delivered in the company. It's a human story, so we'll use the main players' words as signposts as we trace its path.

THE EARLY YEARS

Novell, Inc. has a history that is now well into its third decade, a long life in the world of information technology. Novell Data Systems Incorporated (NDSI) was founded in Provo, Utah, USA in 1979 as a computer manufacturer and maker of disk operating systems. In January 1983, Jack Messman and Safeguard Scientifics, a venture capital firm, reincorporated NDSI to form Novell, Inc., to design and manufacture software and hardware used for networks. In May that year, engineer and marketer Raymond J. Noorda became president and CEO of the new company.

Novell's subsequent history shows a pattern of growth and innovation based both on internal development and acquisition. Novell's early products helped found the corporate network market with the introduction of LAN (Local Area Networks). In 1983, Novell introduced NetWare, the first LAN software that was based on file-server technology. It allowed a business to create a LAN comprised of various PCs and designate one of them to control access to shared devices, for example disk drives and printers. The need for broader, faster, nimbler corporate networks grew fast, and soon wide area networks were the norm. Product development and enhancement continued accelerating in the 80s, so that by the early 90s, Novell's NetWare operating system, adapted for the needs of distributed enterprises (i.e., organizations with multiple locations), led the market with a nearly 70 percent share.

The balance of the 90s saw Novell adapting its core networking products to the Internet arena and launching Novell Directory Services (NDS) to help tie diverse platforms together. In 1999, Novell launched eDirectory, a true cross-directory service that features interoperability and open standards, which are key to Internet use.

KEY ACQUISITIONS

Acquisitions helped shape Novell's present state. In July 2001, Novell acquired the consulting firm Cambridge Technology Partners, enabling it to deliver both services and products to customers. Jack Messman, of Cambridge, became president and CEO of Novell, becoming its CEO for the second time. In July 2002, Novell acquired SilverStream Software, a Web services application developer. This enabled Novell to help customers convert business processes to Web services, using its application platform and identity management infrastructure for Web-based applications.

Novell's acquisition of Ximian in August 2003 opened further opportunities. Ximian was the leading provider of desktop and server solutions enabling enterprise Linux adoption. The acquisition expanded Novell's ability to work with customers using both Linux and Windows environments. Miguel de Icaza and Nat Friedman of Ximian (still at Novell) are known as open source experts; they led two key open source projects resulting in GNOME for the Linux desktop, and Mono, an open source platform for running Microsoft.NET applications.

In January 2004, Novell completed its acquisition of SUSE LINUX, Europe's leading enterprise Linux vendor. SUSE, a German company, brought advanced technology and a Linux customer base to Novell. The addition meant that Novell could offer Linux solutions from the server to the desktop with enterprise-grade networking services and strong technical support.

NOVELL'S CORE BUSINESS

Novell offers enterprise-wide infrastructure software and services. It provides a flexible combination of open source and proprietary technologies. Novell helps its customers manage, simplify, secure and integrate their heterogeneous IT environments at a low cost while increasing the return on their IT investment. As part of its differentiation strategy, Novell also helps customers migrate from proprietary to open source software at a pace that suits them. Novell's customers expect world-class engineering, backed by worldwide support, services, and education, from both Novell and its network of partners.

THE COMPETITIVE ENVIRONMENT

Novell operates in the fascinating world of proprietary and open software. Microsoft, the giant proprietary software company, has dominated the market for years, but now has to take serious account of open source (non-proprietary) software, including Linux, which is free and allows customers to see the programming codes that make them work (thus the name open source). Open source customers don't pay for software licenses; they pay instead for services, including upgrade protection and technical support.

Novell's ability to deliver top-tier customer support services worldwide is therefore a competitive differentiator relative to Red Hat, Inc., and other smaller Linux distributors it competes with. In the broader market, as Linux becomes an increasingly relevant competitor to Unix and Windows, Novell's ability to deliver infrastructure, security, and management solutions that meet customer needs on a flexible, open platform is another competitive advantage. Being able to deliver excellent customer support is a critical element in this capability.

FAST FACTS ABOUT NOVELL

Here are some headlines about Novell.

- Novell's corporate headquarters are in Waltham, Massachusetts, USA. There are more than 100 offices in 43 countries worldwide.
- Regional or development offices are located in Provo, Utah, USA; Bracknell, UK; Nürmberg, Germany; Paris, France; Sydney, Australia; São Paulo, Brazil; Tokyo, Japan; and Bangalore and Mumbai, India.
- More than 5,000 employees work for Novell worldwide. A network of 5,000 partners serves its own customers with Novell support.
- The fiscal year 2004 sales totaled US$1.166 billion.
- Among some 52,000 enterprises, Novell's customers include American Honda, Bank One, Blue Cross Blue Shield, British Telecom, Canon Business Solutions, Cathay Pacific, British Airways, CitiExpress, City of Los Angeles, Lufthansa, Michelin, Nissan, Southwest Airlines, Star Alliance, State of California, Sumitomo Bank, UK Ministry of Defense, Wyeth, and The Washington Post Company.
- Its eDirectory, the basis for security and identity management offerings, is used by more than 30,000 customers, while NetWare, its traditional operating system, is run on some 4 million servers worldwide. ZENworks, a cross-platform management solution, has an installed base of 38 million seats and delivers 3 million applications daily.
- BrainShare, Novell's proprietary conference, started in 1986. A recent one in the US drew about 6,000 attendees, a third of whom had attended for the last five years.

BUSINESS STRATEGY: KEEP AND GROW CUSTOMERS

Not surprisingly, deepening customer loyalty and expanding the business within customers are major growth strategies for Novell. It's difficult to switch providers in the game of enterprise-wide systems, but Novell doesn't want to retain customers just because the switching costs are high. Novell's strategy is to make customers so satisfied with both the technical and the personal aspects of the support they receive that the customers don't consider switching. Also, given the fact that Linux is a free operating system that anyone can download and use, service excellence for Novell's Linux and Open Source customers is especially critical.

WHERE CUSTOMER SUPPORT FITS IN

Customer support at Novell is led by Mike Lyons, Vice President of Novell Global Support Services. The group has about 800 employees worldwide. It is effectively divided into two parts: field and technical support center engineers.

The field engineers (Primary Support Engineers, or PSEs, who each support three to seven customers exclusively; and Dedicated Support Engineers, or DSEs, who support a single customer each) often work face to face with customers and sometimes even have an office at the customer's site. They develop in-depth knowledge of their customers' business. They fit into Novell's business development strategy by providing excellent customer service, but also by consulting with managers in the customer's organization so they can proactively spot business issues that Novell can further support – deepening and expanding business in the account.

Technical Support Engineers, or TSEs, operate in technical support centers and take service requests from other customers. In that sense their work is reactive when contrasted with that of the field engineers. Because they deal with the customer online, by e-mail, or by phone, they must build trust, empathy and credibility without seeing their customer's facial or body language. Of course, they also must have excellent technical skills, but they need to have superb interpersonal skills so they can connect with customers, personalize the service, and ensure a high level of satisfaction.

Whether in the field or in the technical support centers, these engineers' role in Novell's business development strategy is to help customers do their business well, creating value and strengthening loyalty that sustains business.

Novell is organized in six service regions worldwide: Asia Pacific (APAC), Canada, Europe-Middle East-Africa (EMEA), Japan, Latin America, and North America. The regional units can adapt certain practices to their local markets, but since the company is organized to "follow the sun" with customer support, they also must be able to serve customers in the ways their neighboring regions find appropriate. For example, the EMEA technical support center TSEs are busy each morning helping North American customers who need support during the late hours of the night in their local time (see pages 87, 90 and 92 for more on this). It's understood that while there may be differences in procedures, the face to the customer is always consistent regardless of locale.

THE OLD REPORT CARD: ADEQUATE BUT NOT EXCELLENT

In the early 90s, the IT market was undergoing a transition. According to Barry Haug, Director of Novell's Mid-West Area, based in Dallas, Texas in the US, "IT budgets were getting pared down and competition was stiff. Novell faced the challenge of creating a competitive advantage that was strong and sustainable. We asked for customer feedback, and found some interesting themes in the responses. Our technical support was judged to be very strong – it has been highly regarded in the industry for years and was consistently ranked number 1 or 2. We heard, however, that our interaction skills could be improved. In the end, technical excellence becomes a commodity. We wanted something more. So we decided to invest in customer service skills for our engineers."

Dave Cutler, Vice President of Novell Support Services, was already on board. "At that time, managers of the tech support group, some 50 strong, would fight to the death before sending an engineer out in the field. Our support was call-center-centric, which was understandable, given the thinness of our staffing. We were running behind in response time – a typical problem in a growing company. But I mean *really* behind, like a week or two, in replying to service requests."

So although its performance on actual problem solving was excellent, the interpersonal quality of the service was certainly not exceeding customer expectations. Further, the support group was a cost center, like most customer service divisions at the time. And there were problems in the customer service strategy as well. "We were organized around products, not customer types or needs," recalls Cutler.

THE START OF A TRANSFORMATION

The first stage of improvements came with a split in the US's tiny tech support staff's assignments. Some engineers were made available solely for incoming calls. The rest of the team had the difficult task of calling back customers who'd been neglected (think about how much fun that assignment must have been). But it was a much-needed act of corporate courage to accept responsibility for the slow response time, even if it was a byproduct of rapid growth. Dave Cutler explains, "This was before we got started with SigNature Service. But it shows we were already on track to start treating customers like they wanted, even if that meant that existing requests got a somewhat slower response until we dug out of the hole. We began thinking like a customer, who wants to talk with someone now, instead of like a production line, first-in-first-out."

Cutler recalls Mike Lyons' arrival at Novell as the start of a strategic change in direction. Lyons came from Wang Computers, where he had already made changes that resulted in support center profitability. In this regard, the hardware providers were ahead of software groups. IBM makes almost 50 percent of its revenue from services these days ($40 billion of total revenues of $90 billion). But this was innovative thinking even relatively recently.

"Mike did some things that were almost brilliant," Dave Cutler chuckles. Lyons tends to influence by asking questions rather than telling. He considers getting things done his first priority and develops relationships carefully, yet prizes harmonious working relations. He's the kind of guy who wants his facts in hand and the risks clearly identified. On the other hand, he is a hands-off leader.

The major thrust of Lyons' changes was to make NTS field-friendly and customer-friendly. "We placed engineers in major metro areas so they could actually go and visit clients to solve their problems. We gave clients the option of having a semi-dedicated or even a fully-dedicated engineer, but more important, that person became a single point of contact who could get to know our customers' businesses – their needs, goals, equipment and practices."

Revenue from the NTS group reflects the success of this major culture shift: in 1995 the unit produced revenue of some $30 million. But by 2004, its revenue had risen to $140 million, more than quadrupling in less than 10 years. More than 800 people now work for NTS worldwide, including field engineers and technical support center employees. The head count of field-based engineers has grown from zero to nearly 400 in the last eight years.

CHANGING THE SUPPORT SERVICES MENU

The next stage was to upgrade the services customers could get within the technical support centers. The new set-up created two tiers of customers and related service, to address the differing levels of expertise and needs that customers have. "Some customers literally need instructions on where to find a button to push," Cutler explains, "while others are very sophisticated and require a different level of discussion and help. Likewise, some customers prefer transactional working relationships, while others need a long-term, in-depth interrelationship."

Effectively, the foundation of Novell's troubleshooting service starts on the Web. Many customers answer their questions and solve their problems there without needing further support. Beyond that, service is available on an ascending basis, under a contract, like a subscription. Premium 1000, 2000 and 3000 customers can contact a Technical Support Engineer (TSE) and be guaranteed a response within a specified period of time.

Permium 4000 and 5000 service contracts give customers one-on-one contact and the mobile phone number of their designated support person at Novell. This way they can develop a history together, the engineer can

VARIABLE SERVICE LEVELS AND PERSONALIZATION

By making a tiered offering of support services, Novell helps customers choose the level of service suited to their business needs. Notice the increasing level of personalization in the most customized support. Personalized interaction is still part of every customer service contact, but it is noticeably stronger in the higher levels of service. Note: This chart is for discussion and illustration purposes only and should not be assumed to represent Novell's current offering.

Overview of Premium Services Packages

Benefits

				Advantage Support Engineer	Primary Support Engineer	Dedicated Support Engineer	
Dedicated Resources							High Level of Service and Personalization
Account Management			Service Account Manager	Service Account Manager	Service Account Manager	Service Account Manager	
Access	12 x 5	24 x 7	24 x 7	24 x 7	24 x 7	24 x 7	
Technical Support Center Incidents per Year	10	25	50	50	50	50	
Maximum Response Time	4 Hours	2 Hours	1 Hour	1 Hour	30 Minutes	15 Minutes	
Tools and Training	1 Support Resource Library 1 eDirectory Toolkit 1 Education Voucher	1 Support Resource Library 1 eDirectory Toolkit 1 Education Voucher	1 Professional Resource Suite 3 Education Vouchers	1 Professional Resource Suite 5 Education Vouchers	3 Support Resource Libraries 2 Professional Resource Suites 6 Education Vouchers 1 BrainShare Pass	6 Support Resource Libraries 3 Professional Resource Suites 10 Education Vouchers 2 BrainShare Passes	Lower Level of Service and Personalization
	Premium 1000	Premium 2000	Premium 3000	Premium ASE	Premium 4000 PSE	Premium 5000 DSE	

Less Customized Configuration → Most Customized Configuration

Key to abbreviations:

12 x 5	Service 12 business hours per day, weekdays
24 x 7	Service 24 hours per day, every day
Support Resource Library	Support Resource Library support packs, documentation, publications, product documentation
eDirectory Toolkit	eDirectory Toolkit resources for eDirectory implementation
Education Voucher	Education voucher for training
Professional Resource Suite	Professional Resource Suite subscription to toolkits, evaluation, and other re sources
BrainShare	BrainShare passes to Novell's proprietary conferences

learn more about the customer's business and goals, and a partnership develops. Premium 4000 customers have access to a specific Primary Support Engineer (PSE), so they can develop an ongoing relationship with that person, knowing their PSE has only three to seven customers to serve exclusively. Premium 5000 customers have a full-time claim on their Dedicated Support Engineer (DSE), much like having an employee. (See the chart on page 27 for more detail.)

Novell customer support engineers also serve a network of channel partners. A typical channel partner might be a computer systems consultant who has a contractual relationship with Novell for support. The consultant advises, supplies equipment and software, and perhaps manages the IT needs of his or her own client. When channel partners need support beyond the scope of their own capability, they can contact Novell for the services outlined in their contract. The problem-solving function and treatment are the same as for an end-user client of Novell's, however.

Mike Lyons believes that if you provide really excellent support for your clients, they will actually pay for it. When asked how he created the new model, Mike Lyons reflected a moment, then said, "It was really very simple. We discovered that as a profit center, we are better able to fund a higher level of support for our largest enterprise customers."

Barry Haug, speaking of the field engineers, recalls, "We had a window of about 12 to 18 months where we were the only vendor doing this, and it gave us a great opportunity to cement relationships with major customers. We began to see that if we provided an extremely high level of service, the customer would pay for it, stay with us longer, and sustain long-term relationships with Novell. And that was, of course, what we were after."

Chapter Two

Picking a Partner

Picking a Partner

With the vision and goals articulated, it was time for Novell to define the problem and identify a partner to supply the necessary conceptual framework, training, and performance improvement processes and measures that would affect the transformation.

Defining the problem and developing vendor criteria

To kick things off, a project team drawing members from different functions across Novell was formed. They refined their problem statement and also developed criteria by which the prospective vendors would be evaluated. Dave Cutler explains, "We were looking for a consultancy that had a success record with technical support center transformations, preferably in our sector." The specific criteria came down to these:

- The vendor had to have already done significant work in the area of customer support.
- The vendor's references had to be superb.
- The implementation had to be replicable, so that the whole customer support team around the world in both the technical support centers and field assignments could be provided with consistent training.
- The vendor had to be prepared to train Novell trainers ("train the trainer") to help leverage the implementation (this turned out to be done less than expected, but it is still part of the solution today).
- The solution had to be customized to Novell's particular business situation.

THE CALL FOR PROPOSALS

Cutler recalls the consultant selection process. "We initially felt that about ten vendors qualified, and we invited them to develop proposals. We explained that our engineers already had exceptional technical skills, but that even the smartest of them weren't routinely delivering support in the ways the customers wanted.

"Barry Haug, who at that time was a manager living in Provo, Utah (and currently is Director of Premium Services Central Area), was talking to a colleague working at Hewlett Packard in Canada. He learned that Hewlett Packard had recently partnered with Wilson Learning to train some 700 people in their technical support centers all across North America, with excellent results. HP had both field and technical support center support engineers, so Haug's colleague recommended we contact the consultant who helped implement their culture change."

With that referral, Haug contacted Marion Bunch, a Wilson Learning consultant who had worked with Hewlett Packard, and others, to invite them to bid for the project. Bunch recalled, "I understood that at Novell the engineers also were organized in two groups, in technical support centers and in the field. So I was very familiar with the context."

"Customer support is the toughest job in business," states Bunch emphatically. "It's mood challenging. You can assume the person on the other end of the line is calling with a question or a problem and you have a split second to identify the customer's emotional condition and respond appropriately, assuming of course you have the appropriate technical knowledge. I think an important factor in the initial stages of our discussion with Novell was that HP had been happy with our work with them. You know, a happy customer is the best reseller you can get."

Bunch turned out to be an ideal contact for Novell. Not only does she understand customer service in the technology industry, but her previous experiences as a personal assistant to the CEO of McDonell Douglas, business-to-business selling, and her personal commitment to using the tools she provides clients in her own work give her strong credibility with them. She is a partner in Strategy Implementation Resource in Atlanta, Georgia, USA. The firm is associated with Wilson Learning's training and consulting business and has been Wilson Learning's top performing agency most of the years since its inception.

It's an insight into Bunch's character that after the death of her 28-year-old son Jerry from HIV/AIDS in 1994, she turned her loss into a very successful personal cause. Since 1997, she has dedicated much of her leisure time to a personal crusade against HIV/AIDS. A dedicated Rotary member, in 2004 she won an $8.1 million grant for HIV/AIDS work to help orphans and vulnerable children in six countries in Africa. Her volunteer work takes her to the African continent, as well as many other continents, to speak about how Rotary International can respond to the AIDS pandemic.

THE POWER OF DISCOVERY IN PROPOSAL DEVELOPMENT

Bunch is a believer in the Wilson Learning techniques and tools she offers clients. One key tool is discovery. In discovery, a combination of questioning and listening skills along with several other techniques (which we will examine later) help you draw out your customer's goals and the obstacles that keep your customer from achieving them. Bunch is very good at discovery. She uses it consistently in her work. The results help her structure solutions for her clients like Equifax, AXA Insurance, and others. It is a key tool in consulting and sales, of course, but it also has tremendous value for customer service people.

GAP ANALYSIS

Bunch describes the process she followed to develop the proposal. "I phoned several Novell executives, including Mike Lyons, Dave Cutler, Barry Haug, and others, and interviewed them in classic Wilson Learning discovery style. I needed to get an accurate picture, in the executives' own words, of the current situation, plus what they felt the ideal situation would be. Only then could we determine together what created the gap between the two. This Gap Analysis comes straight out of the Wilson Learning sales process, which is called The Counselor

Approach. My Novell contacts could see me using some of the very techniques that we would end up teaching their people, and they could see for themselves how well they worked."

Dave Cutler comments on her approach. "Marion is a master of getting what she wants. Others call her the nicest nagger they've ever met. But it's also true that she has completely assimilated the techniques that end up in the solutions she proposes for clients."

As Bunch completed her discovery process, her Gap Analysis confirmed what Novell's executives sensed: while Novell's support engineers were technically excellent, their support skills (as communication or people skills are often called) were not at the same level. Research with customers confirmed this. Developing the engineers' customer service skills could close the gap.

Bunch resumes the story. "When I had collected my discovery info, I got in touch with Tevilla Riddell, who is the principal of The Riddell Resources, based in Texas. Tevilla has worked with both the Wilson Learning Counselor Approach and Signature Customer Service programs in many organizations around the world. I consider her to be a real guru of customer service at Wilson Learning. Tevilla helped shape the proposal with her in-depth knowledge of these programs plus her expertise in diagnosing customer service problems and solutions. Tevilla and I were equal partners with discrete roles throughout the process."

CREATING A CUSTOM SOLUTION

Bunch also called in Noel Hudson (also known as "St. Noel," in tribute to his patient, persistent method), a highly respected independent facilitator affiliated with Wilson Learning, to help customize the solution. The blend of proactive skills in The Counselor Approach and reactive skills in Signature Customer Service offered a creative approach that addressed the gap revealed by Bunch's discovery work.

Novell received the various vendors' proposals and selected five to proceed with to the next stage. Then they narrowed the field to two.

Barry Haug remembers why the project team finally chose Wilson Learning. "At every stage, Marion, Tevilla and Noel modeled the behavior they were talking about implementing in Novell. They did excellent discovery. They listened. They were the most responsive of the vendors, and they clearly were interested in our business problem, not in selling. And we felt there was an excellent match of corporate values as well. They developed the type of relationship we want to model with our customers. In the end we have invested more in this program than we ever anticipated because they provided such great value and satisfaction. Novell obviously desires the same type of situation with our customers."

ELEMENTS OF SUCCESS

What made the proposal fly? One key to its success was its comprehensiveness, using the Human Performance Improvement (HPI) model. The proposal addressed more than just skills training of the front-line engineers to improve their customer service skills. It also required management engagement. Mangers were to be trained first, then taught how to coach their engineers, so that after the engineers were trained, their new skills could be continuously reinforced and improved. Finally, the proposal envisioned integrating all these transformations in the working vocabulary, performance assessment, and compensation structure at Novell. That way the key concepts, tools and skills would become embedded in Novell's very fabric.

HPI IN REAL TIME

Riddell recalls the first meeting between the Wilson Learning and Novell teams, in which they jointly reviewed data on what needed to be done.

At that time, Novell was measuring support engineers' performance in terms of "incidents closed," the sheer number of customer support requests handled per day. Riddell remembers saying, "If you continue to use these performance standards, then don't even bother launching this

35

program. You need to measure the service in terms of customer satisfaction, not closes."

Dave Cutler replied mildly, "We can change that."

It was a dramatic moment: a huge organization stood prepared to change its fundamental definition of successful customer support. Riddell recalls thinking to herself, "Wow, this is going to be a genuine transformation. They really understand that improving people's customer support skills will be the foundation for Novell's competitive advantage. And they are ready to build on that foundation and align their systems to make the changes stick."

Many organizations would falter, defer or decline to commit to such a complete transformation. Executives and managers often believe that packing people off to a few days of intense training by experts will take care of the problems that keep them up at night. But, as proponents of the HPI model are aware, the most effective change requires these elements:

- **Executive commitment.** Right from the start, executive support was strong. One of the most significant elements in Novell's overall transformation of customer service lay in executives' commitment to do all that was necessary to enable engineers to deliver personalized, satisfying customer service. The fact that Novell's executives completed the classroom sessions before their engineers began was a critical factor in the program's remarkable success. It meant they led by example, not by directive, and continued to embed the program's skills and tools in their own daily work. And they were on hand to kick off every single session around the world, explaining how the program supported corporate strategy.
- **Management alignment.** Managers need to be fully behind the new approach. They move beyond "approving" training, and embrace the full gamut of changes required to support the change that the training simply launches. These can be structural, operational, or attitudinal changes.

- **Management development.** Different from alignment, this means that managers learn, understand, model and fully adopt the world view, skills and techniques their employees will learn, and actively use them in getting their own work done day to day.
- **Employee dedication.** Sometimes this is not a given. Consider that you are an engineer and have been told consistently that you are a master of the technical information your customers need in order to solve their problems. How will you feel when you hear you will soon "get trained" in support skills – people skills, communication skills – if your job satisfaction and all previous measures of your performance were focused on the technical side? You may be intrigued and eager to add new insights and skills to your current bag of tricks. But you could just as easily feel threatened, mistrustful, fearful of making a fool of yourself, out of your depth, and generally not thrilled with the prospect of being asked to do something you don't (currently) value.

Clearly, the message and its manner of delivery were critical to the success of the whole venture. The proposal Novell received from Bunch, Riddell, and Hudson took these issues into account, and made clear that everyone would have to be involved to make such a sweeping change.

DELIVERABLES

Having won the business, Noel Hudson from Wilson Learning worked with the Novell managers to further refine what should be delivered. It would be essential to get the managers involved in customizing the solution, tapping their input and learning precisely what their own concerns would be.

Marion Bunch remembers the creative engagement of the managers as they finished the customization process and moved into the pilot sessions. "Novell really took on the whole package: they branded the programs with Novell-type names emphasizing the big N logo of the company. So the overall initiative was called the Customer Partnership Program, and the customized programs were named Novell SigNature Service and Managing SigNature Service. It was phenomenal to see how well management got behind the effort."

THE FRONTWARD AND BACKWARD APPROACH TO CONSULTING

Marion Bunch uses an unusual approach in her own account management. "I believe in what I call a 'frontward and backward' approach. While we were competing with other vendors, I handled the front work with Novell, doing discovery. Tevilla, Noel, and I worked together to prepare the proposal and the deliverables – the tools, job aids, customized role plays. Tevilla and I presented the proposal together. Later, when we won the business, Tevilla went into action with the implementation. We cast her as the expert, the guru who would work deep in the Novell organization to get results. She made it her business to learn Novell's business inside out, and then combined that knowledge with her expertise in customer support. I was the practical person, the money person, the planner. If questions of scope or money or who-does-what came up, Tevilla would refer the Novell people to me and I'd handle them. Clients say this works well for them, and it also does for us. It frees Tevilla to focus on consulting with the client."

NOVELL'S CORPORATE CULTURE

As we saw earlier, Wilson Learning had been invited to propose a solution for Novell's support group in part because of its successful work with Hewlett Packard's customer support groups. But the Novell culture was also a factor: it is exceptionally open to change. That's perhaps one reason why Linux is a good fit with Novell's core business: It's an open system that encourages creativity and sharing.

Despite the fact that Novell has nearly 5,000 employees in 43 countries and 100 offices worldwide, employees say there is a high degree of trust in the company's leadership and a family-like organizational culture. The company has always prized and fostered a lot of respect and appreciation for learning and education, as well as for high ethical standards and behavior. Indeed, Novell ranked 9th in *Business Ethics Magazine's* "100 Best Corporate Citizens" list once again in 2005.

Many Novell engineers have lived and worked away from their native countries, so they are well prepared to appreciate diversity and the need to be prepared for changes through focused training and learning new skills. "I see that in the classroom," remarks Tevilla Riddell. "We work through a conceptual piece, then change gears and do skill practices or role plays to help imbed the learning in the engineers. In my work with some other clients, skill practice is sometimes met with groans or nervousness. With Novell, the attitude is 'Sure! Let's get started!' There's no fear. You see really unconditional trust. The engineers give each other fantastic feedback, too, and those SigNature Service Checks make the appreciation real."

SigNature Service Checks and Other Reward Systems

In Novell's North American offices (and recently, in others) there's a simple, effective system that engages employees in reinforcing innovation, cooperation, and excellence. Employees are given ten SigNature Service Checks each month, worth a dollar each. When somebody sees a colleague giving exceptional service or wants to thank someone for going the extra distance to help, they can fill out a check, sign it, and give it the colleague. People collect them until they accumulate an amount they want to spend. They can then use them to get gift certificates for things like dinners at restaurants, gifts, and so forth. In the SigNature Service sessions, the checks really fly around as a reward for participation, brilliant comments, etc.

Whatever the reasons, according to Marion Bunch, "Novell was simply readier than other organizations to embrace change and embed it in their way of working. Right from the start it was a fun project. I've never had a client so ready to absorb new ways of doing things. Sure, initially there was a certain reserve, even push-back. The engineers did, and still do, have superb technical know-how, which is shown by the early customer satisfaction scores. But those scores dramatically improved once they added the support skills to help them relate to the customers more successfully. Now those scores indicate nearly complete customer satisfaction. I think the magical combination is their talent and experience, the correctly targeted solution, and Novell's commitment to thorough-going change."

TRAINING SKEPTICS AND SUPPORTERS

CHAPTER THREE

TRAINING SKEPTICS AND SUPPORTERS

In business, as in life, you can view change in many ways. You can see it as a wonderful opportunity or view it as a threat. Your personal outlook, experience, the timing and manner of the change, and the way in which change occurs can all shape your view. Undertaking this huge transformation, the leaders at Novell were highly aware that its success depended on making it a positive, productive experience for everyone involved. It was, after all, part of a key business development strategy.

The Customer Partnership Program rolled out quickly throughout the organization. The managers of North American field engineers began their classroom sessions in April, 2001. Their engineers began theirs a month later. After some additional customization, the technical support center engineers began their classroom sessions in October 2001, despite the disruptions following the September 11, 2001 attacks on US cities. By mid-2002 the global rollout had begun.

SKEPTICAL MANAGERS

Naturally some Novell customer support managers were skeptical at first, in varying degrees and regarding various aspects of the program. Some viewed support skill training as "tree hugging." Some, especially those based outside the US, viewed the approach as "very American" (read: not necessarily going to work here). Others had historical baggage. "We had had the typical 'bad training' experience some time before, where we brought in a consulting firm to improve our performance in another skill. That vendor trained the front-line people without building support from management first," Dave Cutler recalled. "Not surprisingly, the impact was not what we wanted and needed to see."

Brad Palmer, Manager of Novell Support Services, has been at Novell for more than 15 years, always working in Novell's customer support area. "I just find it so appealing," he reflects, "and the team is super. I wouldn't want to work in any other function." Nonetheless, Palmer confesses, "I wasn't too thrilled to be asked to go through that first pilot with the other technical support center managers. I thought, 'This is just more work. It's going to take time away from my daily management responsibilities, and that costs revenue.' I didn't get the big picture. But we went through the course as a team, and we quickly jumped onboard. The time away from our engineers and customers was a necessary but reasonable investment that offered potentially huge returns. And we began to see results right away."

Tevilla Riddell, who has trained the majority of Novell's engineers worldwide, was well aware of Brad's initial take: "I knew that Brad was one of the biggest skeptics before the first session for WSS. I thought, 'Why is he being put on this project? I don't feel the support we need coming from him. He acted like this was one more item to check off on his to-do list. But at the end of the first day of training, he had made a huge turnaround, one of the biggest I've ever seen. He's invaluable in making sure everything is ticking along now."

SKEPTICAL FIELD ENGINEERS – AND CURIOUS ONES

"We engineers are rightly proud of our technical expertise," one remarks. "It wasn't easy to get buy-in from some, who knew they knew their stuff, to commit serious time and energy to develop their support skills."

In particular, in the earliest sessions, engineers pushed back with honest, respectful vigor: "I've been doing a good to excellent job with my customers for 13 years now. I've been to countless tech trainings. And probably one or two support skill trainings, which I don't think I ever got much from. So why pull me off my job for this now?"

Others, like Derek Paxton, a Premium Support Engineer based in Columbus, Ohio in the US, with six years' experience at Novell, felt intrigued. He recalls, "I was glad to see Novell focusing on the customer service aspect of our jobs. As a software company, Novell has always been good at training support engineers in the technical aspects of our jobs, but our customer services skills varied widely from engineer to engineer. It wasn't that we had people with poor customer service skills, just that we had a mix of people with strengths in different areas. Some were able to tell their customers 'no' without seeming unhelpful, some were good at gaining their customers' trust, some were good at clear explanations, etc. But I don't know that there were any that couldn't use help in some of these areas."

Paxton participated in the pilot sessions for engineers. They were true pilots, intended to identify final improvements that could be made to the curriculum before the program was launched officially. And the pilot paid off. Paxton explains, "In the pilot sessions, I could understand the concepts Tevilla Ridell was teaching, but I had to translate them to make them applicable for my own job. At the end of the pilot, we were asked for feedback. I asked that the examples and practices be made more specific to what we do, and that Tevilla spend some time in the field, learning what we do day by day.

"Tevilla responded to this by going onsite with me to work with one of my customers. She spent the day shadowing me, watching me do my job. For me, getting the opportunity to get direct feedback from Tevilla on how I worked was fantastic, but I think it really paid off in giving her material so she could fine-tune the sessions for the rollout. The sessions now feature situations we deal with on a daily basis, so there's no need to translate concepts into application."

As the engineers themselves went through the SigNature Support program and began to practice the skills and techniques they had learned, the effects were immediately obvious. Brad Palmer tells a story about a support engineer he managed who was technically brilliant but rather short on people skills. "It was no more than a week after the guy went through the training that someone sent me an e-mail to let me know about a service request this engineer had handled with exceptionally good customer service skills. And that person didn't know that the guy had been through the course." Tevilla Riddell remembers the turnaround as well. "This was a great triumph, for him and for everyone involved. To this day, the engineer credits his classroom experience with making him a better person. That's remarkable."

THE "YOU MAKE THE DIFFERENCE" CAMPAIGN

Following the initial technical support center training sessions, management met again to discuss what "Aha!" concepts they took away. Palmer recalls, "For me, one huge breakthrough concept was the difference between objective and purpose. Your *objective* is the issue of the moment, like when a customer requests help with a server that's not functioning as planned. Your *purpose*, however, is to help your customer succeed in business – in this case, maybe to be able to access a patient's medical data fast and decide whether emergency surgery is needed right now.

"In the classroom, you hear a little story about people who attach critical body function monitors to premature babies. It really struck me what a world of difference there is between saying, 'I hook babies up to tubes' – an *objective* – and saying, 'I save babies' lives,' the inherent *purpose* of your work.

"Our management team came out of our "Aha" session determined to start a 'You Make the Difference' reinforcement campaign for our engineers. When you think about it, Novell software and service supports emergency phone numbers, airlines, banks – all sorts of organizations that can have a critical impact on people's lives. The difference between one minute and two minutes literally can mean life and death sometimes."

And even if it's not life and death, it can be financially catastrophic if a company loses business due to downtime. Novell advises customers to consider the cost of downtime when deciding what response time they need in their service contracts.

ESTIMATED LOSS OF REVENUE FROM DOWN TIME

The cost of downtime due to software and associated service problems varies by industry. Nonetheless, it's expense for everyone, and it tests customer loyalty if you are a service provider who cannot respond quickly and effectively.

Downtime Cost Per Hour by Industry

Brokerage	$5.6-$7.3 million	Catalog Sales	$60-$120 thousand
Credit Card	$2.2-$3.1 million	Airline Reservations	$67-$112 thousand
Pay-Per-View	$67-$233 thousand	Teleticket Sales	$56-$82 thousand
Home TV Shop	$87-140 thousand	Automatic Teller Machine Fees	$12-$17 thousand

Source: Stratus Corporation

TRAINING AS A TWO-WAY COMMUNICATION

The visible, active presence of management for the actual training sessions sends a clear message of their dedication to the program. Of course they are eager to help the engineers learn. But two aspects of the program also open the training sessions to engineers' input on their work so they can influence change themselves. These features are the Manager on Deck and the Parking Lot.

THE MANAGER ON DECK

Cory Bench was one of the first engineers to go through the SigNature Service training in Provo. "I was really impressed by the commitment management made to improving something that was already good," he recalls. Since then Bench has become a Service Account Manager, then

Manager in a technical support center, and now he's Manager of Premium Services in Dallas, Texas, USA. Recently he was asked to be Manager on Deck for a refresher session of SigNature Service. "You are on hand for the entire session," he explains. "You attend to demonstrate your own commitment to the approach, and you get to be actively involved in the course, supporting the learning and helping people to apply their learning more effectively. I watch and give feedback on role plays, reward and recognize exceptionally good behavior, and then share in wrapping up the course with Tevilla Riddell."

Gemma de Koning, Novell's Service Delivery Manager in the EMEA Services Center in Capelle, The Netherlands, also finds being Manager on Deck a very positive experience. "As it happened for me, I went through the course as a participant, then immediately after that, I served as Manager on Deck for another group being trained. When you take the course as a participant you are focused on learning and practicing. When you get to go through it again as Manager on Deck, your role shifts and you can focus on other people. You actually learn new things about the approach as you watch colleagues learn. You are modeling the behaviors and giving feedback, so you get extra practice too. It was good to get this added perspective."

THE PARKING LOT

All participants are encouraged to feel free to say anything and ask anything – not just about the course content – during the sessions. Sometimes these contributions and questions can't be handled in the course. For example, during Novell's acquisition of SUSE Linux, there were questions about what message should be consistently given to customers.

When such items come up, they are written up on sticky notes and put on a flip chart page on the wall that's headed "Parking Lot." The Manager on Deck is responsible for helping to decide when something should be pursued at the moment or put in the Parking Lot. Then, at the end of the session, the Manager on Deck recaps what's been put in the lot. He or she is expected to "valet" (i.e., deliver) the Parking Lot items to the next management meeting and to get each item assigned for follow-up, reporting the results on the SigNature Support site in Novell's intranet.

"When we began rolling the program out," Tevilla Riddell says, "we'd have 20 to 25 items in the Parking Lot at the end of a course. There would be procedural questions, marketing intelligence, ideas for new marketing messages, suggestions for streamlining things, etc. Gradually each item has been acted on and the outcome reported back, so the participants have had the satisfaction of making changes, getting answers, highlighting new trends, putting items directly before management and posting the answers on the SigNature Service site.

"The Parking Lot enables us to focus on our work at hand during the session," Tevilla notes, "but it also cuts down on whining and emphasizes the accountability of the Manager on Deck. The expectation that Parking Lot items will be addressed makes it a positive, two-way tool for change and improvement."

FROM THE FIELD TO THE TECHNICAL SUPPORT CENTERS

In 2002, 18 months after the field engineers began to be trained, Brad Palmer's boss asked him to be an internal project manager for the SigNature Service launch in the technical support centers. Even though he was aware of the big impact the program had already had on the field engineers, he knew it would take extra work to make it equally successful in the technical support centers at Novell.

Palmer took on the internal project management role with gusto. He adapted what Barry Haug had developed for the North American field engineers, revising the skills taught so they focused on the technical support center's particular demands. He and his administrative support team also developed checklists to ensure each session goes smoothly. Coordination with participants' managers, course materials, food, logistics, guest speakers, hotels, and so forth are all given careful attention.

As an experienced consultant, Tevilla Riddell doesn't underestimate the value of this internal support. "Brad makes sure that everything is prepared and provided – right down to the snacks. That may seem somewhat trivial, but it demonstrates in concrete terms how seriously Novell takes the training days themselves. Brad's support makes it possible for all of us to focus on the learning. And the administrative team that coordinates the training classes, people like Terri Shields, Cynthia Vallencourt, Cheryl Harmon in the US; and Friederike Phielix in Capelle, have all been through the training themselves, so they really know what they are supporting and how it fits in the bigger picture for Novell. This is another example of Human Performance Improvement working in a real world setting."

PROTECTING THE INVESTMENT

Brad Palmer knows how much it impacts the technical support centers to take a person offline for three days of training. "We make it an iron-clad rule that when someone is in the course, they are not allowed to be pulled out, no matter what arises with their customer. I'm proud to say that in all the years we have been involved with SigNature Service, we have never had an engineer pulled out. They and their managers make arrangements for seamless coverage of their customers before the session, and they stick to their plans.

"Tevilla Riddell and I developed two communications that are sent out to managers before a classroom session starts. One goes to managers of participants, and the other to managers who will be a Manager on Deck for that session," Palmer continues. "The letters remind the managers of the importance of the training itself to our strategy. We encourage executives and managers to make time to visit the sessions while the training is going on, and to stay for lunch or a break with the participants to further engage everyone in the effort. We ask a guest speaker to kick off each morning and afternoon session. Vice presidents, directors, managers, and peers of the participants start things off with particulars about how the training fits our larger strategies, or works into daily practice, or just won some new business, and so forth."

Riddell underscores that point, adding, "A VP has started *every*, and I mean *every* US class – sometimes even calling in from vacation on a mountain in Wyoming."

LETTER TO MANAGERS OF PARTICIPANTS

This message goes to each manager who has an engineer due to participate in a SigNature Service classroom session.

Dear World Services Support Manager/Director,

You have one or more engineers scheduled to attend the upcoming SigNature Service training sessions to be held October 15 through 18 in Provo.

As you know, we as a management team must show our commitment to this development of our people in order to reap the long-term benefits it will provide. With that said, I would like to remind you of a few suggestions for you to help demonstrate your commitment to this training process to your employee.

Take some time before the training sessions to meet one-on-one with each employee scheduled to attend. Incorporate some of your own Ben Duffy questions to address some of their concerns. Let them know that this is not "just another training" and that our whole organization will be improving our behaviors to implement what we learn in SigNature Service. Let them also know this is a long-term commitment by Novell and you expect them to give it their all, as you will.

Remind them that everyone in the organization, including you, will be held accountable for displaying the customer interaction skills learned in SigNature Service. Make sure they know that you will be practicing these behaviors as well. Make sure they know you will expect them to practice what they learn once they have completed the training, and that they will be creating an action plan on what they will be doing differently after the training. Encourage them to participate actively and to feel free to say anything.

Commit to them that you will not pull them out of the training for any reason and that you will not expect them to answer their cell phones. Also, commit to being open to their feedback concerning the course or other items and encourage them to give you, the Manager on Deck, or the instructor that feedback. Ensure they know you want to help them and that you too will help coach them on the skills they will be learning.

Some other points:

- Refer them to the FAQs about the training on the Worldwide Support Services Web page
- Remind them that it will begin at 8:00 sharp
- Ensure that you have arranged adequate coverage to meet your commitment of keeping them in training
- Lunch will be served daily. If you have time, drop by for lunch to demonstrate your interest in how the training is going.

It is imperative that we all show a high level of commitment to this training, since it is part of our growth strategy. By communicating this commitment to our employees, we can all speed up the process of implementing what we learn and MAKE THE DIFFERENCE. Please let me know if you can think of anything that I can do to help you.

Brad Palmer

LETTER TO MANAGERS ON DECK

This message goes to each manager picked to be the Manager on Deck in a SigNature Service classroom session.

Dear Cory,

Hello to you. I am looking forward to seeing you this week.

I see that you are up next to be a Manager on Deck and assist with the SigNature Service class, so I want to touch base with you before the classroom experience to help prepare you. You probably have a few questions in your mind already. I'll address them now.

1. How can I help?
Besides modeling the principles of SigNature Service, I will look to you to provide the color commentary as issues come up. Your real world experience will be a great asset in the classroom and provide credibility from the manager's point of view. I will rely on your help to position HOW this training will be implemented, measured and rewarded. Also, I would like you to relay any successes that may be of interest to the participants. Please be prepared to inform the class about what progress had been made (examples will be great). You will also need to introduce the "You Make the Difference" segment related to the concept of *purpose*. Check with colleagues for the latest success story (you may want to speak about the purpose, giving examples and then distributing copies of one of the success stories).

2. What can I do to keep people focused?
I am sure there will be new issues that will come up, so if you can help me get them into the Parking Lot, it would be great. Also, if the class gets stuck on coming up with examples, you can push them, feel free to comment, and keep them on track. Your help in keeping them focused and engaged will also be useful.

In some of the past workshops, we have seen some "customer bashing" by engineers in the class. I will ask the class to rethink what that does to their "self-talk" and treatment of the customer. I will also look to you to tell them to knock it off if they continue.

3. What other things should I be prepared to do?
Other things I need your help with are the two games. We will be giving out SigNature Service Checks so your assistance in reminding people to use them is greatly appreciated.

Also, during the skill practices I will use you as a coach to help the groups practice the skills for improvement.

At the end of the course, we will need your help in the graduation ceremony. This is a good time to ask that each engineer send you what they will be doing differently

LETTER TO MANAGERS ON DECK (continued)

for the next three weeks (it takes 21 days to develop a habit). Ask them to send you an e-mail stating what this will be, and to cc their manager. Let them know that they should follow up with their manager at the end of the three weeks, and ask them to keep you posted as well.

It is also a good idea for you to recapture any relevant information from the class, including the Parking Lot issues.

4. How can I prepare?
Review all of your own course materials so that you are familiar with terminology. Come up with success stories showing how *you* have used the skills, and any changes you have seen in your department with the participants who went through the first session. Review the HELPR process in the Managing SigNature Service book, because when you are coaching during the training, I would like you to use that process to help the groups. I will be listening to you as well as to the groups, so that I can help you get better at using HELPR also. To remind you:

H = Hear them out: focus on having them state what went *well*

E = Expand on the good

L = Listen for *their* suggestions on what to do differently next time

P = Provide additional suggestions (one or two) for improvement

R = Recognize overall positive behaviors.

5. What should I bring?
Yourself! In addition, bring your job aid cards (especially from Managing SigNature Service – it has the HELPR process on it) and the SigNature Service book you used in the content session. Also, we play actual customer calls in the classroom and they are a big help, so make sure you know how to access those calls. Hopefully some new calls will have been added.

6. Anything else I should do before the course?
Please remind the people that report to you to be there ON TIME (8:00 AM). A Vice President is kicking the course off. It is great to have managers drop by the sessions, so encourage others to come by – even just for lunch!

Thanks in advance for your help,

Brad Palmer

THE OUTCOME: FULL PREPARATION FOR CHANGE

When you step back from the individual pieces of the puzzle, the bigger picture emerges: Novell takes its responsibilities seriously, ensuring that the climate and follow-through for the program is correctly executed, leaving little to chance and bridging just about every potential obstacle that could lessen the impact of the classroom sessions and their application on the job. Let's take a look now at what actually goes on in the classroom portion of the solution.

CHAPTER FOUR

LEARNING KEY CONCEPTS

CHAPTER FOUR

LEARNING KEY CONCEPTS

The classroom component of the overall solution at Novell is fascinating in its own right. After all, we are all customers of other organizations, so we are "experts" in what makes good and bad customer support. But are we conscious of our expertise, and do we use it effectively? This chapter will no doubt make you more aware of your own expertise, and very likely will enlarge it.

As we have seen, all of Novell's engineers and managers completed the Novell SigNature Service program. Managers also received special training on coaching and managing their engineers in a second program, Managing SigNature Service. It helped to reinforce their learning and ensure the training became a way of work for everyone – with a strong emphasis on how to model the learning in their own work, day by day. Everyone involved agrees that this strong, ongoing management commitment to embed these programs has been a major factor in their success.

Since the field engineers support one to three customers per person, they often work face-to-face and can play a proactive role in expanding and deepening Novell's business with them. In contrast, the technical support center engineers don't see their customers in person. They focus on resolving a particular service request to the customer's satisfaction, and while some problems may take a month or more to resolve, they do not expect to develop an ongoing relationship with each customer they help. So a lot rests on their ability to quickly develop trust, credibility and empathy, again and again.

This chapter will provide a brief view of some of the elements of SigNature Service and Managing SigNature Service. It's not possible to capture the experiential learning that happens, but these key concepts will give you an idea of the content.

SigNature Service

At its core, the SigNature Service approach says that a Novell customer support engineer *can* make a difference in each customer contact. As they progress through the program, engineers analyze what they actually do in the service chain linking Novell's services, products and strategies with its customers; how they interact with customers; and what impact they have on customers and on themselves.

A key segment teaches engineers how to manage themselves and handle the inevitable stress of their role in difficult situations. A process called the Customer Satisfaction Approach gives them specific ways to think and act in order to create and sustain customer satisfaction. To do that well, however, they need to be good – and quick – at identifying a customer's current emotional condition and what needs and expectations that customer brings to the contact.

The goal is that upon completing the course, engineers are able to consistently achieve higher levels of customer satisfaction, expand their "toolkit" of skills so they can handle customers in a wide range of situations successfully, and increase their own personal and professional effectiveness.

The SigNature Service program takes place over three days and includes brief presentations, video and audio tapes, role plays, group work, practice and critical observation. Most examples and role plays simulate typical situations the engineers run into in their work.

The entire experience helps engineers learn "from the inside out," which means they make the learning part of their way of working, so much so that it seems to be the most natural way of doing things. At every session there's active, strong input from the Manager on Deck (see pages 52-53), who connects the content to Novell's strategies and critical success factors regarding customer support: to increase and sustain customer satisfaction, loyalty, and thus improve revenue growth.

CONSCIOUS AND UNCONSCIOUS COMPETENCE

Many engineers found the classroom experience a refreshing reinforcement of their natural ways of working. Jim Sumsion, a Worldwide Support Engineer (WSE) based in Provo, Utah in the US, has nine years of experience at Novell. "My introduction to SigNature Service fit like a comfortable glove," he recalls. "I've always treated my customers like I would like to be treated, but the classroom sessions gave me names for things I try to do, and therefore made me more conscious of what I was doing. For example, I have always tried to ask and answer any key questions I think my customers may have, before they do so. I learned that's called the Ben Duffy Technique."

Wilson Learning would call a person like Sumsion an "unconscious competent" when he started his training. His comment above shows him gaining "conscious competence." By becoming conscious of his natural ways of supporting customers, Sumsion could strengthen them and also see where he could add new skills or techniques.

THE BICYCLE MODEL

Wilson Learning is famous world-wide for its Bicycle Model. It's a simple, almost elegant way of explaining how technical and people skills interact.

- The engineers are invited to consider the parts of a bicycles they metaphorically apply to the skills needed for excellent customer support.
- Their back wheels, which power the bike, are strong. Back wheels represent the engineers' technical skills: their product, policy and procedure knowledge.
- Their front wheels, which of course balance and guide the power of their back wheels, represent people skills: the ability of an engineer to show patience, courtesy, empathy, good communication, and

friendliness. This aspect had not been emphasized or developed before by Novell.

- Their gears represent the engineers' flexibility – their willingness and ability to shift between technical and people dimensions during an interaction, depending on what the customer's need is. Engineers need to become self-aware so they can make good judgments on the fly.
- And finally, their handlebars, which steer, remind the engineers that they can control and manage their own emotions so they can manage each customer contact successfully.

THE BICYCLE MODEL FOR FRONT WHEEL AND BACK WHEEL SKILLS

We tend to think of skills as a large set of things we know how to do. But it's helpful to distinguish between the technical and people skills we use from moment to moment.

Job/Technical (Back wheel)	Technical job skills, product knowledge, knowledge of policies and procedures
People (Front wheel)	Patience, courtesy, empathy, good communication skills, friendliness
Flexibility (Gears)	Willingness and ability to shift between job and people dimensions, depending on the customer's needs
Self-Management (Handlebars)	Willingness and ability to control emotional response in order to manage the interaction positively

THE OPPORTUNITY CALCULATION

Early in the first day, the engineers calculate their opportunities for impacting customers, both internal (within Novell) and external, and then multiply their daily numbers to see what that means per week, month, and year. They see they have a wealth of opportunities to make successful impacts if they make the right choices.

PURPOSE AND OBJECTIVE

Unless you've consciously considered the distinction, you might use *purpose* and *objective* interchangeably when you talk about someone's work. However, in terms of customer service it's very important to distinguish between the two: the engineer's purpose is to support the customer's business success and make money for Novell, while the objective is to handle particular service requests or problems successfully so customers can succeed in their business and continue to choose Novell over any competitors, and help the engineer reach his/her performance requirements.

SATISFACTION AND THE ZONE OF INDIFFERENCE

Satisfaction refers to a customer's internal judgment of the quality of an interaction with an engineer. The notion of satisfaction itself is complex, since satisfaction and dissatisfaction are not opposites, but two discontinuous scales that apply to the event. Research by Wilson Learning has revealed a "Zone of Indifference" where dissatisfaction and satisfaction are *both* relatively low. These customers are neither very satisfied nor dissatisfied; they are simply indifferent. They are important to consider and treat with extra care, because an indifferent customer is a customer at risk to be lost to competitors.

The fact that satisfaction is an internal judgment is tricky: It means that your customer may not say how (dis)satisfied he is with the interaction unless you ask. Thus each interaction should include a moment when customers are prompted to say how satisfied they are. If they can be moved out of the Zone of Indifference toward satisfaction, it's an important step toward long-term business growth.

THE ZONE OF INDIFFERENCE MODEL

We tend to think of customers as feeling either dissatisfied or satisfied, in one extreme or another. However, if you picture the two as discontinuous scales, there's a gray zone, the "Zone of Indifference," where both satisfaction and dissatisfaction are low. Customers in the Zone of Indifference are highly vulnerable to the appeals of competitors. And since they feel indifferent, they very likely won't volunteer clues on how they feel. It's very important to get a customer to say how satisfied he is – because you may not know unless you ask. Having a customer in the Zone of Indifference isn't necessarily a bad thing. They are engaged with Novell but not loyal. The goal is to win their loyalty.

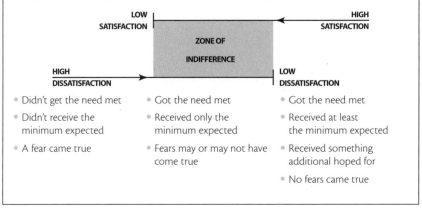

• Didn't get the need met	• Got the need met	• Got the need met
• Didn't receive the minimum expected	• Received only the minimum expected	• Received at least the minimum expected
• A fear came true	• Fears may or may not have come true	• Received something additional hoped for
		• No fears came true

SIGNING YOUR NAME

Think for a moment about the last time you experienced exceptional service. It probably had several characteristics:

- It met or exceeded your expectations, even surprised you.
- It was personally significant to you.
- It might not have cost the service provider a lot.
- It will make you remember the service provider.
- It involved the person doing something better, more personal for you.

Novell engineers learn that if they pay close attention to the customer as an individual, are committed to the customer's satisfaction, are easy to deal with, and provide service they are proud enough to sign their name to, they will consistently gain high satisfaction ratings. That translates into customer loyalty, which is a huge competitive advantage for Novell. And that also makes the engineer feel satisfied.

SELF-MANAGEMENT

Customer service can be highly stressful at times. Partly that's because the focus is frequently on solving problems that are preventing customers from getting their business done. Partly it's because customers don't always feel obliged to tell you you've done a good job. And if they are dissatisfied, they may voice it in pretty unpleasant ways – or just go away. A lot is on the line with every interaction. So managing your side of the equation gives you a much better chance of a successful resolution, and gives you a good shot at feeling satisfied with your work.

Early in the training session the engineers work through an exercise that helps them to manage themselves better. They learn that an event – in this case, an interaction with a customer, or even just a moment in that interaction – triggers a perception within them, a sense of how things are going contrasted with how they think things *should* go. This perception can describe the event in any number of ways: it is the engineer's "self-talk," his internal conversation with himself. Feelings result from the self-talk, and ultimately, his behavior reflects those feelings. It all happens in an instant, much of the time unconsciously. The trick is to get more conscious about it and to manage it for maximum positive effect.

THE ROLE OF FEARS IN SELF-TALK

In a challenging situation, one of four typical fears is often activated: a fear of making mistakes, of failing, of being rejected, or of being hurt. However, even though a fear is activated, self-talk can make a big difference. Consider how the various kinds of fears can be coped with and corrected by changing focus, as shown on page 64.

SELF-TALK AND FEAR

The key to handling various kinds of fears successfully is in managing them through a change of focus.

Dimension	Type of Fear	Negative Self-Talk	Change of Focus	Positive Self-Talk
Job	Fear of Mistakes	"I must always be right."	Self-Worth	"I can learn from my mistakes."
Self-Management	Fear of Failure	"I must always win."	Growth and Learning	"I don't have to lose in order for someone to win."
People	Fear of Rejection	"Everyone must like me."	Win-Win Attitude	"My self-esteem isn't based on how many people like me."
Flexibility	Fear of Pain	"I must always be comfortable."	Willingness to Adjust	"My discomfort is temporary; I'm willing to adjust."

STOP-CHALLENGE-FOCUS

It's one thing to grasp this concept, another to break habitual behavior. To do so, Novell's engineers learn to recognize when they are acting from habit. Then they apply the technique called "Stop-Challenge-Focus." It's a simple but effective way to move to positive self-talk and act productively.

When engineers recognize they are responding from habit, they mentally interrupt the conversation. Literally taking a deep breath (or several) gives them time to do this. They then challenge themselves and ask, "What am I telling myself? Is it true? What's going to happen if I act on this self-talk?" Finally, they ask themselves, "What do I want to happen? How do I want to act? What do I need to tell myself so I can achieve that?"

Brad Palmer tells a story that illustrates this point. "Recently I was discussing the performance of one of our engineers during his year-end performance review. We talked about how he was practicing Stop-Challenge-Focus in his own work. This person has a fairly short fuse, but using the tool, he has made great strides in this area. He told me that he absolutely dreaded having to go to the class and kept his negative attitude through most of it, mostly because he felt like he had better things to do. However, he decided to give the tool a try. Now, two years later, he has integrated the skills and continues to use them to improve."

THE CUSTOMER SATISFACTION APPROACH

The Customer Satisfaction Approach creates a schema for each customer interaction. It has four stages, but the second and third ones should be considered a loop that gets repeated until the customer expresses satisfaction. The four stages are these: Open, Interact, Ask for an Expression of Satisfaction, and Conclude.

THE CUSTOMER SATISFACTION APPROACH

Each customer interaction is a sequence with these stages. If each stage is handled successfully, the outcome should be a satisfied customer, nearly all the time. Note that the third stage, where a support person asks for an expression of satisfaction, may actually trigger a "loop" that gives the support person added opportunities to develop a more satisfying solution.

	OPEN	INTERACT	ASK FOR EXPRESSION OF SATISFACTION	CONCLUDE
Actions:	• Identify condition	• Determine needs and expectations • Meet needs and expectations	• Ask for an Expression of Satisfaction	• Thank • Follow-up
Skills:	• Self-management • Observation • Establish rapport • Personalize	• Listen • Question • Empathize • Explain • Say no • Adapt	• Patience • Persistence • Sensitivity	• Personal warmth • Professional follow-up

---

OPENING

In the Opening stage, Novell's engineers learn to establish rapport, identify the customer's emotional condition, and personalize the contact. They must quickly determine the feeling the customer is bringing to the contact: Is the customer comfortable, irate, insistent, or indecisive? Watching a video sharpens the engineers' ability to diagnose the customer's condition quickly. They then listen to a tape of real calls from Novell customers to give them specific examples. These recorded calls are updated frequently so the material stays current.

Each condition has specific traits and requires specific treatment.

- If the customer is comfortable, the engineer can reinforce the condition by expressing appreciation: "I appreciate your good humor, even though this must be frustrating to you."
- If the customer is irate, nothing much can be gained until the customer's anger is validated: "I can see/hear you're angry, and I can understand why." Then the engineer must pause, to allow the customer to vent.
- If the customer is insistent, the engineer understands that moving to take action is going to be most effective: "OK, let's get this fixed."
- If the customer is indecisive, then reassurance and clarification are called for: "That's what I'm here for. I'll explain what you need to do, step by step, and stay on the line until you have it working properly again."

At the same time, the engineer may need to use the Stop-Challenge-Focus technique on himself, especially if the customer's condition touches one of his personal fears that still triggers habitual responses.

RAPPORT

Regardless of the customer's condition, the engineer won't get too far toward solving the problem without establishing rapport. Rapport works positively for both parties. The customer begins to feel more comfortable and to trust that the engineer is willing to help. The engineer feels tension lower as the personal connection grows, making room to work on the solution in a positive atmosphere. Rapport is established differently depending on whether the contact is face-to-face or over the phone. The first moments are critical.

- On the phone, engineers are taught to greet the customer, introduce themselves, and make it clear they are willing to help. They don't interrupt, but keep a close focus on the conversation and what the customer is telling them. Of course, they clearly acknowledge the customer's condition ("I see that's important; let me ask you to give me a moment while I review your service request.")
- When dealing face-to-face, the engineers start with a smile and look up or approach the customer, establish and keep eye contact, greet the customer, shake hands and introduce themselves. They listen and acknowledge the customer's condition ("I can help with that. Let's review the log of these transactions and see if we can find the source of the problem.").

PERSONALIZING

We all enjoy service with a personal touch, something that's specifically done for us. For Novell engineers, it's also a source of satisfaction that lets the engineer put a personal signature on the service they provide (hence the name of the program, SigNature Service). Personalizing service becomes a source of personal and professional pride for the engineer. For the customer, it also distinguishes the service as a special benefit of dealing with Novell as a provider.

So personalizing has two aspects. First, the engineer makes a point of respecting the customer as a unique person – using his or her name; demonstrating a personal interest in the customer's business; making an effort to anticipate the customer's related or future needs; volunteering additional tips or advice; and whenever possible, presenting options or

CUSTOMER CONDITIONS AND INITIAL RESPONSES

THE COMFORTABLE CUSTOMER

Verbal Cues

Pleasant/friendly
- Uses phrases such as "Uh-huh"
- Responds quickly to the provider's acknowledgment
- Thanks the provider for service

Conversant
- Chats with the provider
- Responds to questions/ comments
- Greets the provider
- Listens to the provider

Cooperative
- Offers the information requested
- Gives complete/additional information
- Accepts the provider's statements

Relaxed
- Waits for the provider to finish speaking or doing the task
- Speaks in a calm, unhurried voice

Nonverbal Cues
- Laughs, smiles
- Nods agreement
- Makes direct eye contact
- Shows relaxed body posture
- Leans toward the provider; hands may be in pockets

Recommended Initial Response

Appreciation. Show the customer that he or she is valued.

THE IRATE CUSTOMER

Verbal Cues

Insulting
- Spits out words
- Makes "You..." statements
- Swears
- Makes accusations

Intimidating
- Speaks loudly
- Doesn't listen
- Interrupts
- Threatens
- Abruptly puts the provider on hold or hangs up

Confronting
- Requires proof
- Uses stern, hard tone
- Expresses certainty: "I know I'm right."
- Uses condescending phrases

Argumentative
- Interrupts
- Speaks loudly, quickly
- Is sarcastic
- Repeats points of argument

Nonverbal Cues
- Scowls
- Leans forward
- Pounds fist
- Stares the provider down
- Shakes finger
- Makes direct eye contact

- Has stern, superior facial expression
- Shakes head from side to side
- Uses exaggerated gestures

Recommended Initial Response

Validation. Let the customer know it's okay for him or her to be angry. Listen and allow the customer to vent his or her emotions.

CUSTOMER CONDITIONS AND INITIAL RESPONSES

	THE INSISTENT CUSTOMER	
Verbal Cues	**Assertive** • Initiates conversation • Asks direct questions • Sounds very confident about responses to the provider's questions **Directive** • Explains in detail • Uses well-chosen words • Has everything ready before asked • Makes suggestions	**Demanding** • Speaks very quickly, with few pauses • Uses short sentences **Abrupt** • Uses clipped, fast-paced speech • Uses incomplete sentences • Doesn't engage in extraneous conversation • Interrupts • Answers questions quickly
Nonverbal Cues	• Moves toward provider to gain attention • Follows provider as he or she moves • Stays in close physical proximity • Checks watch or clock	• Points finger • Moves quickly • Drums fingers on counter or desk • Taps feet • Frowns
Recommended Initial Response	**Immediate action.** If possible (and appropriate), do what the customer asks.	

	THE INDECISIVE CUSTOMER	
Verbal Cues	**Puzzled** • Mumbles • Ends sentences with questions • Answers with "I don't know..." • Speaks slowly, in short sentences **Hesitant** • Barely acknowledges greeting • Pauses before answering questions • Pauses between words and phrases • Consults with partner • Uses lots of "ahs..." and "umms..." • Seems unable to find necessary information	**Apprehensive** • Seems slow to respond • Has shaky voice • Sounds nervous and uncertain • Speaks quietly **Avoiding** • Seems slow in responding to questions; offers no response • Does not tell provider what he or she wants • Uses defensive statements, such as "It's not my fault."
Nonverbal Cues	• Cocks head to the side • Scratches head • Frowns • Has a blank facial expression • Fidgets	• Shuffles; shifts weight • Makes indirect eye contact • Has a fearful expression • Has tense body posture • Leans away
Recommended Initial Response	**Reassurance and clarification.** Say that you will clarify any information that is not clearly understood. Reassure the customer that you will stay with him or her until their needs are met.	

alternatives so the customer can make choices. At the same time, though, the engineer reinforces that this is the way *Novell* does things: He or she thanks the customer for the opportunity for giving Novell the business (using Novell's name).

CREDIBILITY + EMPATHY = TRUST

With rapport established, it's time to build trust. Trust draws on empathy and credibility. When an engineer shows empathy, the ability to see things from the customer's perspective; and credibility, the know-how, resources and actions that make a difference, a customer's trust in the engineer grows. Quite logically, his sense of risk diminishes. The higher the risk, the greater the need for establishing empathy and credibility.

THE BEN DUFFY TECHNIQUE FOR BUILDING TRUST

A famous technique that Wilson Learning teaches to people in all aspects of business is the Ben Duffy Technique. It's named after an enterprising advertising account executive who eventually became president of BBD&O, a major advertising agency. He consciously put himself in his prospective client's shoes – and won the business.

The story goes that Duffy was considering various approaches to gain credibility and trust from a new prospect. He discarded the traditional approach of parading the capabilities and achievements of his firm by the prospect, and instead asked himself, "What questions will my prospect have in mind?" He drew up a long list of questions and then answered them one by one. Next day, he began the presentation by saying, "As I prepared for our meeting today, I was thinking you probably have a number of questions about me, my company, how we work, and so forth. So I would like to begin by answering them. Would that be OK?"

The prospect smiled and pulled out a list of questions he'd prepared and said, "Let's compare our lists." The match was extremely close, trust was established, and eventually Duffy's firm won the account.

Questions that the customer may have before an encounter may be about the engineer, or Novell, or how Novell does business. Typical Novell customers have questions like these:

- Is Novell able to solve my problem/answer my question?
- Is this engineer experienced enough to handle my call?
- Does this engineer have enough "clout" to get things done?
- Is he really open to my needs, both right now and in the long run?
- What has been done since the last time we talked?
- What happens if he can't fix my problem?

THE PURPOSE, PROCESS, PAYOFF (PPP) TECHNIQUE

Sometimes the customer service engineer initiates a contact, whether face-to-face, by phone, or by e-mail. The Purpose, Process, Payoff (PPP) Technique is both remarkably simple and very effective in getting off to a positive start, and it reinforces the engineer's credibility considerably. It's related to the Ben Duffy Technique in that it anticipates what is probably on the customer's mind, but it also frames the contact and points it toward a productive conclusion. (See pages 51-53 for letters that use these techniques.)

- The purpose statement tells the customer why you are making contact or meeting.
- The process statement tells the customer how you'll proceed.
- The payoff statement explains the benefit for the customer and you.

Derek Paxton, a Premium Support Engineer, tells a story about PPPs and Ben Duffy questions in action. "When Tevilla Riddell was shadowing me to gather material for our classroom examples and role plays, she joined a conference call we held. Its purpose was to introduce an engineer who had just been assigned to support one of my accounts to my contact. The engineer had already gone through SigNature Service sessions. The Novell manager who set up the call started it off by talking about some of the customer's former issues and work that was currently going on. The customer added some details, and the conversation began jumping around from topic to topic, making it more of a casual conversation than a meeting with a set agenda.

"Then the new engineer was introduced. He began by clearly stating why he was on the call, what he was going to talk about, and why the customer would benefit from that (a Purpose, Process, Payoff statement, or PPP, in class lingo). The call became organized and everyone ended up feeling like it had been a good use of time.

"The new engineer also was aware that the customer might be feeling uncomfortable about the transition of support from me to him. He asked and answered his own questions about what he felt the customer would be wondering about him, starting out by saying, 'You are probably wondering what my experience is. Well, I have...' These came from what Tevilla taught us: They are called Ben Duffy questions. Needless to say, Tevilla was very impressed by the engineer and still teases the manager about not starting out with his PPPs and Ben Duffys, to this day."

Determining needs and expectations with listening, questioning and empathizing skills

At a practical level, customer service can never work unless the service provider really understands what the customer's problem is. As we have seen, Novell's engineers have strong "back wheel" knowledge (see page 60), but many found that their "front wheel" skills in the areas of listening, questioning and empathizing were substantially improved by their experience with SigNature Service sessions. A good deal of this was accomplished by active practice with fellow participants.

Needs are what a customer *must* have; expectations center on what the customer would like to have. In some ways these two terms deal with back wheel and front wheel aspects of the interaction. The need may be for information or for action; the expectation may be more focused on the invisible report card they are filling out about how they were treated. Specifically, a customer's need might be to get the server running again. His or her expectation is that it shouldn't be necessary to jump through hoops to get this problem solved. So after an interaction, customers ask themselves:

- Did I get the minimum service I expected?
- Did I get anything more than that?
- Did I get anything I didn't want, or did some fear come true?

DISCOVERY AGREEMENTS

Novell's engineers interact with customers in a variety of ways, but all contacts are documented, often with a discovery agreement. In a discovery agreement, the results of careful questioning, listening and empathizing are shaped in a verbal or written format that follows this pattern:

- The current status
- The desired status
- Task and personal motives (if you had this, what would it do?)
- A request for the customer's agreement to the accuracy of the points as reported
- A recommendation for the next step

Discovery agreements don't have to be long, laborious projects. With practice, anyone can get good at doing them verbally to wrap up any significant phone call, or writing them up quickly in an e-mail following a meeting or conversation. They can be quite informal. Of course, for a high-profile issue or opportunity, a discovery agreement should be fully developed and checked, but the process is the same.

EFFECTIVE EXPLANATIONS

Novell's engineers are so well versed in their technical knowledge that it can be tempting for them to "tell all" and overload a customer who is really only after the solution to his current problem. So in SigNature Service, the engineers get help on making effective explanations. In essence, an effective explanation focuses on the main point or points the customer

---

SAMPLE INFORMAL DISCOVERY AGREEMENT

As you can see, a discovery agreement need not be a fancy, long document. However, it's an extremely effective tool for making sure everyone is working with the same facts and assumptions.

Greeting with Personalization

Dear Sarah,

Thanks for taking time to talk with me today. I hope your office move goes smoothly and you are up to speed again soon.

Purpose, Process, Payoff statement

I'd like to recap what you told me to make sure I understand your situation so we can solve this problem quickly and not cost you down-time.

Current Status:

Currently only some of the sales reps who should be able to access their sales figures can get data through your sales reps' portal. Those who don't have access are unable to prepare proposals and that's costing you revenue.

Desired Status:

Short-term, we need to authorize the reps who can't access the data to get temporary passwords so they can continue their sales campaigns. We can do that in an hour. Then we can take the time we need to find the bug in the underlying code that is blocking them. We agreed that I'll come back to you by next Thursday with our findings.

Request for agreement

I hope I've summarized our discussion correctly. Please make any additions or corrections you want and e-mail them back to me as soon as you can.

Recommending next step

Then, based on your input, I'll go to the next step and get started on the two solutions above.

Warm regards,

Julie

---

needs to know, delivers the information in the simplest language possible, and shows the customer what benefits will follow. In the training sessions, the engineers pick something to explain and develop a script that meets these criteria. Each one presents it to a partner and gets feedback on the same criteria.

SAYING NO

Perhaps in an ideal world, a customer support person would be able to say yes to every request, but that's just not so. Saying no effectively, however, both addresses the reality and can reinforce customer loyalty, interestingly

---

DISCOVERY AGREEMENTS IN ACTION

Derek Paxton, a Premium Support Engineer, finds discovery agreements a real asset in his work with customers.

"The discovery agreement has been a lifesaver for me. I'm a techie, and I always want to quickly get to the issue and get it solved. I used to assume too much and chase down the wrong trail, or spend time on something that didn't matter much to my customers. The discovery agreements are a formal or informal process that makes sure everyone agrees on the future steps that will be taken. Basically, after discussing an issue with a customer, I now summarize the results of the conversation by making three statements:

1. What the issue is
2. What I am going to do
3. When I am going to get back with the customer

"Then I ask for the customer to confirm all three are right or to add and correct anything I've missed.

"These statements can be formally written, e-mailed, or just stated as a way to summarize a call. But they make sure that the customer and I are on the same page and agree on what is going to happen next. They feel more comfortable that the issue is being handled as they require, and I spend less time working on things that are not important to the customer."

---

enough. The Novell engineers learn to discern two dimensions of an interaction: the task and the emotion. Addressing the task requires the engineer to say what *can* be done, outlining any options available instead. Managing the emotional dimension draws on the engineer's self-talk and empathy skills. This enables the engineer to help the customer understand why a particular policy exists, including its benefits. The engineers develop a list of possible replies when the answer is no.

- Here's what we can do.
- We can do X even if we can't do Y.

- I need to check with our team about this. May I put you on hold or call you back? ... Hi again, I've checked with the team and we can get the temporary passwords to you by Monday and fix the coding bug by Thursday. Will that work for you?

Adapting toward the customer

There are times, of course, when Novell's engineers can't change things as customers would like. But they learn to explore how they might adapt company policy or even themselves to the customer. Sometimes they can partially deliver the items needed, with the balance due by a certain date. Or in a crisis, they might not explain how they are solving the problem, focusing instead on the essential information the customer needs immediately, and returning later, if necessary, with a full explanation.

Naturally, all of this requires the support engineer to have a good understanding of the customer's needs: which ones are urgent, which ones need a long-term solution, etc. Moving toward the customer rather than asking the customer to come toward the engineer requires a good understanding of where the customer stands at the moment and rests on good questioning and listening skills as well as technical know-how.

Asking for the customer's expression of satisfaction

You might think that solving the customer's problem is the endpoint for a typical interaction with Novell's engineers. But actually, they learn that it's important to find out if the customer is fully satisfied before the interaction ends. If it isn't, they have the opportunity to make it more satisfactory, either then or in the future.

Asking for an expression of satisfaction need not be a formal, tedious process. It can be as simple as asking:

- Are you satisfied with these arrangements?
- Does that answer all of your questions?

- Did you get what you wanted/needed?
- Are you pleased with the results?
- Are you sure that this solution will be OK, even though you asked for something different?
- How do you feel about this solution – will it work for you?

If the answer is positive, it's time to reinforce that response ("That's great. Thanks for doing business with Novell." "I'm glad you think so." "I'm happy we could help you.")

WHAT IF THE CUSTOMER IS NOT SATISFIED OR SEEMS INCONSISTENT?

Sometimes an engineer does not get a positive response, or a customer says yes but means no when it comes to confirming satisfaction. It's time to go through the Interaction loop again and try to meet the customer's needs and expectations better. (See the model on page 65.) Going through the loop again, engineers can ask:

- Is there anything else I can do now that will make you more comfortable about this?
- Is there anything I can do that will make this more convenient for you?
- Is there anything else we should consider before confirming the arrangements?
- Do you have any additional questions or concerns about this?

Even after asking these questions, an engineer may get the sense that the customer's satisfaction isn't complete. It is time to judge then whether the customer will be irritated by a final attempt to get at satisfaction. If it seems reasonable, the engineer can try the following approaches:

- I sense some hesitation. Are you sure there isn't something else I can do to help?
- I sense you're a little frustrated. Is there something I could to make this arrangement more convenient for you?

- It seems I've missed something important to you. Are you sure there isn't something else I should have covered?
- It is really important to me that you leave feeling satisfied with our service. Are you sure there isn't something you would like me to change?

CONCLUDING AN INTERACTION

Think of the conclusion as a mirror image of the opening of an interaction. In the beginning, engineers are establishing rapport. At the end, they try to establish a feeling of comfort, setting the stage for their next interaction with the customer and beginning a track record for positive, personalized service.

There are a number of techniques that Novell engineers learn to use in the concluding phase:

- They thank the customer for doing business with Novell.
- They offer an appropriate name and phone number or e-mail address for further follow-up.
- If an interaction ends in referring the customer to another person, they consider following up later to see that the customer's needs were met.
- If they transfer a customer, they explain to both the customer and the new contact why they are transferring. They share the information already gained so the new contact has all the critical information and the customer doesn't have to start over. They give the customer their own name and contact info in case the transfer fails.
- They restate who'll do what by when.
- They offer to call back and see how things are going with the solution.
- They reassure the customer that Novell will support him or her, and remind the customer about the service he or she is entitled to under the current service contract.
- Finally, they tell the customer they enjoyed working with him or her (or, when necessary, that they regret the solution isn't fully satisfactory), and look forward to the next contact.

USING THE CUSTOMER SATISFACTION APPROACH
FOR DIFFERENT CUSTOMER CONDITIONS

Here are some ways that Novell engineers vary their behavior in different stages of the Customer Service Approach, depending on the emotional condition of their customer.

CUSTOMER CONDITION	SELF-TALK	OPEN	INTERACT	EXPRESSION OF SATISFACTION	CONCLUDE
	Set yourself up to be:	Greet and then begin:	Determine and meet needs and expectations by:	Ask for it by:	End positively by:
Comfortable	Supportive, appreciative, sincere, accommodating	Showing appreciation and willingness to work with him/her	Showing you care about the person's specific situation	Requesting positive feedback explicitly	Thanking the customer on behalf of the organization
Indecisive	Patient, supportive, nonjudgmental, reassuring, calming	Building rapport to reassure; offering clarification and personal attention	Asking closed questions to clarify; listening; confirming understanding; then acting	Making sure all is clear; things work out (following up if needed)	Reassuring that you're still available later if they need you
Insistent	Cooperative, efficient, confident, assertive, ready to act	Building rapport by showing you'll act quickly	Empathizing, clarifying, offering options (and what you can do instead if you can't do what they want)	Asking if you did what the customer wanted or needed	Offering to be responsible if it can't be done now, thanking them if it can
Irate	Committed to problem solving, managing the interaction; staying calm, not taking it personally	Listening and validating, representing your organization	Empathizing, letting them vent while you stay calm, avoiding defensiveness and excuses or tuning out	Acknowledging the anger, asking if the solution has taken care of the problem	Offering ongoing contact or support

RECOVERY SKILLS

You are familiar with the scenario: some sort of mistake or malfunction creates a real problem for you. In that case, if your customer service person handles the situation successfully, you often come away feeling better about the provider than you did before. Novell's engineers learn recovery skills which help them serve customers in such situations and help return them to satisfaction. They follow a pattern in which the key words happen to start with the letter *A*:

- Acknowledge the situation and the problems it is causing
- Apologize for inconvenience or discomfort caused
- Accept personal responsibility on behalf of Novell
- Adjust things to solve the problem
- Assure that the solution leaves the customer satisfied, checking back later if needed

THE STILL-DISSATISFIED CUSTOMER

Happily, a customer who simply cannot be satisfied is pretty rare. Yet there are inevitably situations where Novell's engineers can't fix a problem to the complete satisfaction of the customer, or where the customer simply refuses to let go of anger or disappointment. In these cases, self-management is vitally important. The engineers learn several methods of self-talk to help balance themselves. They learn to:

- Recognize that some customers may never feel fully satisfied, because of particulars beyond the engineer's control
- Review how they handled the situation, and take pride in having done their very best, even if the customer didn't agree
- Use Stop-Challenge-Focus to interrupt negative self-talk
- Take a break, talk, or even vent with a colleague, out of earshot from all customers, recalling the customers they have satisfied in other cases
- Avoid taking things personally

Above all, the engineers learn that they must re-balance their minds before dealing with the next customer. It's a professional obligation to take a deep breath mentally and then say, "Now on to the next call."

Other skills and models

In the course of the three days the field engineers learn many other specific skills and practice them on one another. They do specially customized role plays based on typical Novell support situations to practice the skills they need to learn in order to handle customers' needs successfully.

In one case, one engineer plays the role of a Primary Support Engineer (PSE) who is meeting for the first time with a customer, played by another engineer. They each have secret scripts, which the third engineer, the observer, is given as well. The customer has been very satisfied with his previous PSE, who has been promoted after two years of good service. In addition to being disappointed about losing his PSE, the customer faces a tight budget next year. If the PSE uses all the right skills – the Purpose-Process-Payoff and Ben Duffy Techniques, the trust-building skills, and so forth – then the customer is permitted to give the PSE important information he needs to expand the business for Novell. If not, the customer will simply not cooperate in the discovery process. The observer tracks the interaction so he can supply objective feedback to both of the role players. A debrief after each role play helps draw out the lessons learned by all of the participants.

Programs for the managers

After they complete the standard SigNature Service sessions, Novell managers participate in special one-day training sessions to help them coach their engineers so that the skills learned in classroom sessions will be reinforced and improved with daily practice. These sessions engage the managers in shaping the practices that will help them accomplish this critical goal. They do role plays and discuss what barriers might hinder changing behavior – theirs and the engineers'. They come up with their own ideas for reinforcing the learning, like SigNature Service Moments and recognition programs.

If you glance back at Brad Palmer's letter to future Managers on Deck (see pages 52-53), you will notice that he explicitly asks them to review their Managing SigNature Service materials before joining the upcoming session for engineers. He writes, "Review the HELPR process in the Managing SigNature Service book, because when you are coaching during the training, I would like you to use that process to help the groups. I will be listening to you as well as to the groups, so that I can help you get better at using HELPR." HELPR is an acronym for key coaching skills that the managers developed. The process prompts managers to give positive feedback to the employees and thus reinforce the use of the new behaviors. When working with an engineer, managers are reminded to:

- H = Hear them out: focus on having them state what went well
- E = Expand on the good
- L = Listen for their suggestions on what to do differently next time
- P = Provide additional suggestions (one or two) for improvement
- R = Recognize overall positive behaviors

As you can see, Palmer is reinforcing the manager's coaching skill while reminding the manager to coach their engineers. The approach is significant enough that the managers have job-aid cards to help them consistently apply the process. Tevilla Riddell also gives each Manager on Deck special help to improve their coaching skills as they carry out their responsibilities for their session.

It was thanks to the management sessions that several other successful reinforcement tools emerged. Brad Palmer recalls, "Tevilla Riddell, who was leading our session, asked us to identify areas where we thought we could have the most impact. One thing we wanted to do was to define our purpose as it relates to Novell's customer support strategy (this is where the 'You Make the Difference' campaign originated). Another was defining who our customers are. We broke into groups to explore ideas and then got back together and presented to the whole group and decided on the direction. The group working on defining who our customers were came back with a chart entitled 'Who Cares?' Their point was that we need to use these skills with everyone we deal with: internally, externally, personally, etc."

Managers learned in their sessions that it is critical for the success of the SigNature Service program for them also to model the same skills in their own daily work. Today, when you talk with these managers, you see how delighted they are with the results, as both they and their engineers use discovery agreements; set up calls, meetings, and e-mails with PPPs; and discuss what stage they are in as they follow the Customer Satisfaction Approach with customers. The ongoing use of all these techniques moves the training from being an event to being a stage in a much larger, high-impact process of integration.

MAKING THE PROGRAM YOUR OWN

In the end, each of Novell's managers and engineers ultimately took in all these tools and concepts and made them their own. And that seems to happen quite naturally. Derek Paxton, a Premium Service Engineer, volunteers, "What I really like about the training is that it didn't include any procedural requirements. We weren't given any scripts to run through, and nobody attempted to make sure we are acting the same way and saying the same things. Instead we were given a bunch of ideas, like tools for our tool chest. We have been allowed to stay flexible, to adapt to our customers' needs, and to draw on the skills we learned in the class as we feel we need them."

Jim Sumsion concurs. "SigNature Service doesn't try to change your personality. It gives you a framework and shows you how to capitalize on your strengths by becoming conscious of them. Of course it also helps you improve in areas where you do have weaknesses. And it's adaptable – you make it your own by putting things in your own words, not becoming a robot.

"Tevilla Riddell, our classroom consultant, modeled the SigNature Service techniques excellently herself, listening carefully, personalizing her interactions with each of us, reading each person's 'customer condi- tion' and responding appropriately. When I introduced myself on the first day, I mentioned that I use pack goats to carry my stuff when I go hiking in the mountains. I mean real, four-legged, two-horned, cloven-footed, cud-chewing goats. Three days later, Tevilla wove something about pack goats into a role play, and we all had a good laugh. In doing that, she illustrated how personalizing your interaction makes people feel good and improves your relationship.

"I find the principles useful at work, but also in every other aspect of my life. I don't use the terminology with my kids, but I model the behavior with them and they pick it up and use it too. And I'm much more sensitive to the good and bad customer service I receive or observe outside of work."

THE END RESULT

The sense you get when you talk with Novell's support engineers, managers and executives about their experience in learning to use the SigNature Service tools and techniques is remarkably consistent: they are as proud now of their people skills as they were of their technical knowledge a few years ago. In the end, the combination of the two gives them greater satisfaction as they consciously advance Novell's strategies.

INTEGRATING:
EXPANSION, REINFORCEMENT,
AND MEASUREMENT

CHAPTER FIVE

INTEGRATING: EXPANSION, REINFORCEMENT, AND MEASUREMENT

As a global company, Novell follows the sun with its customer service. A caller requesting support may not even wonder where the support person is sitting, and in a way, it shouldn't matter. But executing this strategy worldwide, among varied markets, cultures and time zones, is an intriguing challenge. Rolling out the SigNature Service program beyond North America was necessary to support Novell's follow-the-sun service commitment, and it required consideration of local customer needs and expectations worldwide.

Novell has also developed an extensive reinforcement program to ensure that it gets the full benefit of its support skill training investments and the strategies they support. Refresher courses and performance metrics all support the integration of the initial training. Let's look at some aspects of these challenges for delivering excellent customer service.

GLOBAL EXPANSION OF THE PROGRAM

"We started this program in 2001 with the North American PSEs [Primary Support Engineers]," Dave Cutler explains. "Eighteen months later we brought in the North American technical support center engineers. In 2002 we began the worldwide expansion of the program. Consistency is extremely important to our success strategy. Now all our engineers work from the same base of skills, attitudes, and performance, regardless of their location or culture."

Tevilla Riddell has worked with cultural diversity experts at Wilson Learning to adapt the materials used in the global rollout so they mesh well with local cultures. She has continued to lead workshops for engineers and provides refresher courses in SigNature Service skills, but she also trained and certified Carl Palme to deliver the programs. Palme, the India Support Center and Geographical Area Support Manager, is a Californian who has worked on the building phase of Novell's India Support Center in Mumbai (Bombay). He has trained Novell's engineers in Singapore, Australia, and Hong Kong, beginning in the summer of 2005.

"We all face interesting cultural challenges in delivering SigNature Service programs in various markets," Palme explains. "For people born in India, Singapore and Hong Kong, an American accent can be difficult to understand. In the course, I speak as clearly as possible, and a bit slower than usual, but I also emphasize visual and tactile learning. I write lots of things down on the flip charts, so if someone can't catch a key word as I say it in my accent, they can recognize it on paper. Our group in India is a 100 percent technical support center, and it actually supports the North American and Asia Pacific (APAC) markets rather than intra-India customers at the moment. So conditioning their ear to an American accent probably has some value for our people there, apart from the content itself."

"I find our participants from Singapore, Kuala Lumpur, Thailand and Hong Kong are overly respectful and harder to draw out about their work with customers. And they didn't initially use the Parking Lot, although that got easier as time passed. Australians, on the other hand, are blunt and egalitarian – they don't hesitate to say 'This segment is boring' if that's what they think, and they throw an issue on the table with the same vigor. All of these groups find that some phrases suggested in the course materials are 'overnice Americanisms' that would sound weird in their cultures. I encourage them to make adaptations based on what they feel each customer needs based on his condition and culture, but always to stay within the concepts of the program."

Palme noticed that Australian engineers, who on the average had been working for Novell for much longer than some other groups, were reluctant at first to admit a need to develop their support skills. "I found I had to slyly teach those guys – be sensitive to their initial discomfort." He used a technique that Tevilla Riddell recommended, putting modeling clay out around the training room and encouraging people to play with it while they discussed the course content. "They made marbles, snakes, and little villages as they talked. You could see the tension and pressure dropping."

The APAC engineers Palme trains in SigNature Service find the concept of identifying the customer's initial emotional condition amusing table talk at first, but before long they are using it to share examples of their insistent, irate, indecisive and comfortable customers. Regardless of where they come from, however, the engineers are very positive about what they learn and begin to practice it immediately when they return to work.

CULTURAL DIVERSITY IN EMEA

In EMEA (the Europe-Middle East-Africa unit), there is rich ethnic diversity both within Novell and among the customers it serves. Novell's ranking regarding diversity ties it for fourth place among the top 100 Best Corporate Citizens of 2005 in *Business Ethics Magazine*.

One example of the impact of diverse nationalities is demonstrated in the EMEA region. With about 200 employees (including approximately 50 engineers in technical support centers and about the same number in the field), it is Novell's second largest service region, with employees in 11 countries. Gemma de Koning, a Service Support manager at the Capelle, Netherlands office, comments, "Even though our technical support center engineers here in The Netherlands work fluently in their primary and at least one secondary language, there is always the possibility of unintended miscommunication in both directions. We ask a lot of questions to ensure clarity and prevent misunderstanding.

"The differences in cultures across Europe are very significant, and they are important to take into consideration when you provide customer services here. The beliefs and behaviors affected by culture are still very much alive and strong. It is important, for instance, for a Dutch engineer supporting a French customer to be aware of the stereotypes that might come into play, and to understand the culturally based views that might be operating beneath the surface of the conversation. This phenomenon affects the way you manage people in our diverse workforce as well. I currently manage a team that includes German, Danish, Belgian, British, Dutch, Slovak and American colleagues. Nevertheless, good customer service is good customer service, and it has a universal component: a warm, fuzzy feeling for the customer, whatever the content is."

VARYING EXPECTATIONS ON DELIVERY

Other differences have to do with customers' expectations about how support should be delivered. Technical support center engineers handle between 15 and about 30 interactions with customers each day. The customers are often IT managers or experts who have tried but not been able to resolve the question themselves. Novell's technical support center engineers may have many service requests open (i.e., being worked on) at a given time, but they are expected to resolve at least one service request per day on the average. Some problems can be resolved in a few hours; others require months and lots of communication with the customer. But the process flow varies somewhat in different parts of the world.

In North America, 90 percent of Novell's customers begin by using the phone to request support, while the balance request service on the Web or another means of contact. The phone-in customers are accustomed to staying on the line while the engineer works on an answer, or they have contacts with several engineers who work on the service request until the problem is resolved. This is true of Australians as well.

In EMEA, only 40 percent of the service requests come in by phone, usually after the IT expert at the customer's site has exhausted all of Novell's web-based solution tools. Instead, about 55 percent of EMEA customers request service via the Web. Either way, an incoming service request is logged in by a customer service representative, who opens a file, inputs the technical data, routes the request to a product team, and confirms with the customer what will be done by what time. The file notes the level of service and response time the customer is entitled to receive according to their service contract.

Whether they contact Novell by phone or the Web, this procedure means EMEA customers do not stay on hold. They can go about their business during the guaranteed response time. Igor Zotkin, a service delivery manager in the Capelle, Netherlands office, explains, "In our view, support is overdeveloped in North America, and customers have become conditioned to expect that. It costs customers time on hold, and it costs Novell more overhead. Here in EMEA, our customers are aware of the level of service they have subscribed to and they are satisfied as long as we respond within the time frame their contract specifies, which we do 95 percent of the time. Our approach allows an engineer to develop a solution or action plan and return to the customer, often earlier than required, without the hold time and many back-and-forth calls we see happening in North America.

"It's a difference in market expectations. In North America the competition in the marketplace is much more focused on fast, phone-based response, and customers believe they are gaining time by staying on hold. We are perfectly able to provide service this way, and we do it every day from 8 AM to 2 PM here in Europe when we cover the night shift North American calls. But our customers favor a different approach for our markets here."

OTHER CULTURAL DIFFERENCES IN CUSTOMERS

Marc Cordes, a German customer service representative in the Capelle, Netherlands office, sees some cultural patterns among the customers he helps. "Germans often want action – now. They don't like to read information on the Web page; they prefer a personal guide to troubleshoot with them hand in hand. They are very conscious of response time and tell you if you're a minute late phoning back. We try to educate them so they can solve future problems themselves, but I sometimes think of a saying we have in German: 'If you give them a finger they will take your whole arm.'" Akos Szechy, a Hungarian technical support engineer who is also based in Capelle, says his German customers are notably interested in knowing *why* something works in a certain way. "They also want to test the possible solution in a lab environment if their issue is critically important. It can be much more challenging to build trust with a German customer than with some others."

British customers often call up and begin immediately to describe their problem, not introducing themselves or their company. They seem to be less flexible in participating in the solution, but they do what you ask them to do to get there, according to Cordes. "They, plus the Germans and the Dutch, seem most interested in getting the most service they can for the least expense."

With these and countless other influences, it can be a real test of agility for the Novell support teams to treat customers the way they want to be treated and get to a solution efficiently, as well. Rodrigo Gomez, an Argentinean technical support engineer, says, "I just put myself in the customer's position and recognize their emotional condition. Then we can get started on a solution."

Another factor that comes into play is fatigue, according to Gomez. "Sometimes a morning call here in EMEA comes in from a technician who's up in the middle of the night somewhere in North America. He may have been trying to fix an urgent problem without sleep for the last 24 hours. Some of these customers are literally in a panic, not able to concentrate well, and actually tell us their job is on the line. That can be very demanding, but we do our best to get them what they need. It's a slight twist on the idea of customer condition."

REINFORCEMENT

The success of Novell's transformation is integrally tied to reinforcement. Dave Cutler distinguishes between two stages of learning. "Frequently our engineers say their work with customers is transformed overnight following SigNature Service. But they get better with ongoing practice, so we do a lot to reinforce the training as well. Training without reinforcement is an event. Training with reinforcement starts a sustainable growth process."

"We have what we call a 'SigNature Service Moment' at our team meetings, where we make a point of using the content of the course to talk about a specific service request or customer condition," says Jim Sumsion, a WSE based in Provo, Utah in the US.

Derek Paxton, a Premium Service Engineer, sees a payoff in all this. "In our general team calls, from time to time we review and discuss a concept or tool from the class as it applies to our own work. The calls help to remind us of our learning. Thanks to the classroom sessions and then reinforcement, we all use a common language to talk about customer service issues. We recognize when a meeting is meandering because we haven't done a Purpose Process Payoff. We understand what's going on when we are about to shy away from an issue because we don't comfortable taking ownership of it. We are able to say to each other, 'Why are you trying to talk to him now? He's irate, so just listen and don't take it personally.' That shows how what we learned gets used day to day."

CREATIVE APPROACHES TO REINFORCEMENT

Novell's managers are charged with driving reinforcement of the skills in their engineers by modeling them themselves, using them daily, and coaching improvements, thus aligning everyone in the program. They use the terminology from the programs consistently to describe where the engineer is in the support process, what emotional condition the customer was in initially, how satisfied he or she was at the end of the process, and so forth.

Brad Palmer, the internal project manager for SigNature Service in the technical support centers of North America, clearly delights in creating new approaches to reinforcement. "For example, we have a board on our intranet and we post notes about the best SigNature Service performance we see. Each quarter a theme from the program is highlighted. Our engineers have mouse pads that are designed so you can insert artwork changeably. We give them a new graphic or tip from the program about every quarter. We've made little job-aid cards that fit on the back side of people's ID badges, and we hear that in the middle of a call, our people will flip their badges over for a quick reminder on how to handle something. We've got posters up around the office that point to key concepts in the training. We can see that all these things have a cumulative effect, making SigNature Service a way of life."

THE "YOU MAKE THE DIFFERENCE" CAMPAIGN

Palmer and his fellow managers also interview customers to get stories about how Novell software and service actually affect people's lives. The stories are posted on the SigNature Service intranet and are changed frequently. "We use the site to post Frequently Asked Questions (FAQs) about the use of the concepts and tools in the course. We share success stories, tips and tricks that worked particularly well to ensure customer satisfaction, and so forth. We post SigNature Service Moments, stories that highlight a single skill in action in the real work of our people." Palmer sees the engineers drawing on the SigNature Service Moments to shore up their learning over time. "In performance reviews, I often hear that people are continuing to improve the skills they learned in the classroom because we review them in our team meetings. It just helps people buy into the approach and keep the momentum going."

He also makes sure the managers of engineers learn what each engineer will be doing differently for the three weeks after their training, knowing it takes that long to develop a habit. He encourages the managers to follow up with their engineers at the end of the three weeks.

"All our support engineers are fully trained now in these skills. Gradually, through attrition, we are hiring new folks. We run a class per quarter to get the new folks up to speed as quickly as possible, and until that happens, we see that they are mentored in the basics. Unlike some of the experienced engineers who initially felt there was no need to have support skill training, our new hires say this approach to customer support is the coolest thing they've ever seen. They love the idea that we are investing in their success and giving them training so their support skills are at a par with their technical know-how," concludes Palmer.

As the global rollout continues, reinforcement methods that work in one region are spreading to others. Igor Zotkin posts success stories on the performance board in the EMEA Service Center in The Netherlands. Recently Carl Palme's group began using SigNature Service checks in the India Support Center, and they periodically hold SigNature Service special events like award dinners. "In APAC they give out RACE (Recognize and Celebrate Employees) checks and there is a SigNature Services trophy given out quarterly."

Lorin Jenson, director of customer service for Novell Japan, worked with Wilson Learning's Tokyo office to deliver SigNature Service in Japanese to about a dozen technical support engineers and two service account managers. "We try to use the training learned on a daily basis when working with customers," he notes. "In addition, we review a different core skill and practice it in our weekly team meetings. It has been extremely helpful in allowing my team to build and develop long-lasting relationships with customers."

REFRESHER COURSES

Since virtually all engineers in Novel Technical Services have been trained in SigNature Service today, the company has embarked on refresher courses worldwide. Carl Palme says, "We come in knowing everybody uses the basic principles and practices, but we share challenges, sharpen our skills, and help people move into even better mastery of the content. I delegate someone in each section I facilitate to supply local examples. It's a great way to further imbed the training in our daily work."

During refresher sessions, Novell's field engineers also learn how to perform a Gap Analysis with their customers so that Novell can provide solutions and create new revenue opportunities for itself. As we saw earlier, this is the technique that Marion Bunch used to identify what Novell's executives felt were the key problems that needed to be solved to execute the strategy of deepening customer loyalty and expanding business within customers. In their Gap Analysis, engineers ask customers to describe

ALIGNING MESSAGES AND ACTIONS

Not only do Novell's customer support engineers and their managers work with a consistent set of skills and tools. The language and content of the training programs are reflected in Novell's Web site and corporate publications.

Discovery

"We help you assess your current IT investment in the context of your most pressing business challenges, and work closely to identify, prioritize and justify your technology investments moving forward." [Source: Novell corporate Web site]

"We deliver services ranging from one-day Discovery workshops to strategy projects and solution implementations... [Source: Novell corporate Web site]

Advocating and Support

"Novell didn't just sell us software, but was also present throughout every phase of the project, including post-implementation. In times of crisis, which are common during implementations of this scale, Novell sent us the best professionals and spared no effort to overcome our challenges...Novell has gained the confidence of our people. Novell keeps its promises: the company does what it says it will do." [Source: Waldeck Araújo, CIO of Brasil Telecom in *Connections Magazine* May/June 2005, page 11]

Ben Duffy Technique

"Naturally, you are probably concerned about a number of issues associated with open source such as realistic cost benefits, return on investment, impact on business operations, skill sets, training, and support." [Source: Novell corporate Web site]

the current and desired states, and then focus on what constitutes the gap between the two. This helps them identify new opportunities for service.

PERFORMANCE MEASURES

Dave Cutler recalls, "Before partnering with Wilson Learning, we evaluated the engineers' performance on how many service requests they

---

ALIGNING MESSAGES AND ACTIONS (continued)

"We've loaded this issue [of *Connection Magazine*] with several articles to bring you up to speed on the many announcements Novell made at Brain-Share in March. We also answer some of the questions you might be asking yourself about those announcements." [Source: Rob Kaine, VP Product Management in *Connections Magazine*, May/June 2005, page 1]

"Did you find what you expected on the customer's page? Let us know how we are doing by sending an e-mail to customer@novell.com. [Source: Novell corporate Web site]

Consultative Approach

"Together, we help you with more choices than ever before. Our clients tell us we are easy to work with because we focus on solving their problems, not on pushing a particular technology."

"I've been in this business for more than 20 years and have never experienced the kind of partnership like the one we have with Novell." [Source: Dave Lind, Director of Business Systems, Allina Hospitals and Clinics, in *Novell Report*, Second Quarter 2005, page 5]

Personalization and Choice

"Premium Service is a tiered model of service that allows you to select the level of support that makes the most sense for you and for your business." [Source: Novell corporate Web site]

"Depending on your relationship with Novell, the Customer Care portal will give you a personalized view of various tools allowing access to the information you need." [Source: Novell corporate web site]

---

resolved in a period of time. But that method of measurement didn't support the connection to the customer's problem and a satisfactory response to his or her needs. Now we have transformed the performance measures to include a satisfaction index. That helps us check on the individual engineer's use of the skills in appropriate ways that get the results we want in the bigger picture."

USING EVALUATION METRICS TO REINFORCE LEARNING

What is striking about this evaluation form, sent to each customer upon the resolution of a service request, is that it so closely follows the SigNature Service approach and checks on the engineer's use of the program's tools and skills. It's a good example of integrating measurement with the training and definitely reinforces all the key behaviors, while giving an index on the primary objective: satisfaction for the customer.

NOVELL TECHNICAL SUPPORT ENGINEER (TSE) EVALUATION

Name: (Confidential)
Score: 100.00

Evaluator: (Confidential)
Date/Time: 28 October 2005
Incident Number: 12345

Questions in Section 1 are worth 1 point, questions in Section 7 are worth 7 points, Section 8 has the points listed, and all other questions are worth 4 points. Out of 115 points possible, 100 is the expected score that all Technical Support Engineers should get.

	Yes	No	N/A	
1. Greeting				
a. Did the TSE identify him/herself?	✓			ESTABLISHING RAPPORT
b. Did the TSE identify his/her support group?			✓	
c. Did the TSE identify the customer?	✓			
2. Interacting				
a. The customer condition was	Comfortable*			THE FOUR CUSTOMER CONDITIONS
b. Did the TSE respond appropriately to the condition?	✓			
3. Needs and Expectations				LISTENING AND QUESTIONING
a. Did the TSE use Responsive Listening, Restatement, and/or Checking Questions?	✓			LISTENING
b. Did the TSE ask appropriate questions to gather sufficient information?			✓	QUESTION TYPES
c. Did the TSE demonstrate an understanding of the customer's viewpoint, showing empathy?	✓			EMPATHY

NOVELL TECHNICAL SUPPORT ENGINEER (TSE) EVALUATION (continued)

	Yes	No	N/A	
4. Managing the Interaction				
a. If there was an explanation, was it effective?	✓			EXPLANATION
b. If the TSE cannot do exactly what the customer wants, were options provided?	✓			SAYING NO
c. Did the TSE demonstrate flexibility in handling the customer's demands/requests?	✓			FLEXIBILITY
5. Asking for an Expression of Satisfaction				
a. Did the TSE ask for an expression of satisfaction?			✓	SATISFACTION
6. Concluding the Interaction				CONCLUSION
a. Did the TSE conclude the interaction in a comfortable and positive way?	✓			
7. SigNature Support				
a. Did the TSE attempt to exceed the customer's expectations in some way?	✓			EXPECTATION
b. Did the TSE provide SigNature Support by allowing the customer to be able to speak without interruption?	✓			
c. Did the TSE provide SigNature Support by personalizing the service?	✓			PERSONALIZING
8. Overall Performance				
a. Rank the TSE's overall SigNature Service Performance (worth 40 points)	[score = 40: good performance]			SIGNATURE SUPPORT

* Comfortable/Irate/Insistent/Indecisive

Mandatory comments from TSE:

The communication was complicated by voice delay. Personally I feel I should be giving more time for a customer like this one to speak. I felt I interrupted on a few occasions, maybe due to anxiety. The Customer also interrupted me but when his interruptions came I managed to give him time to speak.

I guess I need to be a bit slower in my communication, but it depends on the voice connection.

Cutler continues, "Our performance measures also now include a full 360-degree evaluation, taking into account not just the manager's appraisal, but also customer satisfaction scores and peer evaluations. One key metric is how many service requests were resolved to customer satisfaction. It used to run around 50 percent. Now we run at about 90 percent."

When a technical support engineer resolves a service request, an outside vendor called Satmetrics e-mails the customer a short survey, which clearly follows the key points of the SigNature Service program (see a sample on pages 98-99). Dave Cutler explains, "If we don't see our engineers actively using the skills and tools from SigNature Service, they are put on warning. We take it that seriously."

Brad Palmer adds, "We have revised our performance measures so they track the skills and behavior the engineers learn in our training. As you know, if you don't measure something, it doesn't get done."

GAP SCORES

One of the measures Novell has used to track customer satisfaction with the field engineers is called a gap score. After an incident is resolved, Novell's customers are asked to use two metrics to evaluate a variety of characteristics of their support engineer's performance – responsiveness, technical skill, helpfulness, follow-up, etc. The customer rates the importance of that characteristic from zero to ten, and then, again on a zero-to-ten scale, rates how satisfied he or she is with the way the engineer is performing in that area.

The difference between the importance of a characteristic and the engineer's rating is called the gap score, and the lower the gap score, the better. So for example, a customer may say that responsiveness has an importance rating of eight for them and their engineer is performing at a level of seven. That would produce a gap score of one (the difference of eight minus seven) in that area. If an engineer's performance is rated higher than the importance, then they will actually get a negative gap score (a very good thing). The current industry standard for a good score (which translates into loyal customers) is actually one or less.

Derek Paxton explains, "We measure gap stats instead of straight ratings because it helps even out different interpretations of ratings by customers. One customer may rate an engineer as a seven, thinking someone who does everything just as it should be done would rate a ten, so he means he isn't satisfied with his service in this area. Another customer may consider a seven to be an excellent rating, assuming that a five means average service. So for him, a seven means much greater satisfaction than for the first customer."

Novell's gap scores vary around the world but all are far better than industry standards. The score for North American engineers is less than one. Regarding engineers in India, Carl Palme says, "Our gap scores are around 0.30 now, and the trend is toward lower numbers, meaning we have more and more highly satisfied customers." In EMEA, it's actually been negative (meaning customers are super-satisfied) for more than three years. Every Monday, the EMEA group's data on calls closed and satisfaction scores gets posted for all to see.

According to Dave Cutler, "For the 2005 North American surveys, 90 percent have given Novell's engineers an 8, 9 or 10 – these are called 'Top Box' ratings. We are also looking carefully at the 'raw scores,' because a zero gap score could be generated by having an importance score of 2 and a satisfaction score of 2, which we wouldn't like to see. We are working now to increase the survey responses in the 'Top Box' range."

Customer loyalty surveys done quarterly and semi-annually in various regions also show extended retention, renewals at higher levels of service, and increasing satisfaction as well. It appears through all these metrics that Novell's customer support strategy is being executed very successfully.

EXPERIMENT AND CONTROL GROUPS

Igor Zotkin had an opportunity to informally test the impact of the new training on engineers in the early days of the EMEA implementation. As the program rolled out, engineers were selected more or less at random to go through the training. This produced a control group, which hadn't yet been trained, and a test group, which had. The test group's gap scores were consistently 0.5 points better (i.e., lower) than the control group's scores. Furthermore, when Zotkin interviewed the trained engineers three months after their training, he asked about satisfaction, self-confidence, and stress in their work. They reported increased satisfaction, greater confidence, and less stress. This seemed to be partly because the SigNature Service process requires an engineer to ask the customer for an expression of satisfaction at the end of the interaction. Very few requests lack this positive closure now.

Carl Palme tracked the same pattern among engineers who had and hadn't yet received training in APAC. The gap scores showed a noticeable improvement in customer satisfaction during and after SigNature Service training in the region.

RETURN ON INVESTMENT

All of these efforts help ensure that the considerable cost and energy that go into training, refreshing, and aligning the organization around these principles and techniques repay Novell – but more important, they repay Novell's customers with superb support.

Brad Palmer tells a story that illustrates return on investment in real terms. An urgent service request came in from a person working with a customer who didn't have a service contract with Novell, so it was escalated to Palmer. The customer needed to have something fixed, right then, that would enable him to complete a critical proposal. Palmer reflected on his own SigNature Service training and decided to provide the service on a one-time basis for free. Soon thereafter, the customer returned with good news: the proposal was accepted. "That customer signed an agreement with Novell for US$ 1.8 million a year in product and support, including a Dedicated Support Engineer. The Dedicated Support Engineer was an add-on to the proposal as a direct result of the way we responded to their urgent request. This single case repaid our investment by far more than the cost of SigNature Service training here at Novell. And it's just one case."

CHAPTER SIX

LESSONS LEARNED

CHAPTER SIX

LESSONS LEARNED

It's not easy to make significant change happen in a large organization. Nor is it easy to sustain new ways of working. But Novell's experience in transforming its customer support unit demonstrates that significant, sustainable change is possible when conditions are right. So what key lessons can we take away from this story?

THE HUMAN PERFORMANCE IMPROVEMENT MODEL WORKS

When we began, we considered the HPI model. In Novell's case, every aspect of that model was taken into account as the project evolved.

- The *business drivers*, competition with other open source and proprietary software companies, were articulated clearly.
- Leaders at Novell were explicit about the *strategy* of making excellent customer support a driver for market differentiation as well as for expanding business with existing customers and acquiring new ones, and employees at all levels could articulate how their work supports it.
- Important *information* about the then-current situation (scores showing engineers with superb technical skills but weaker customer support skills, performance measures about the number of incidents resolved rather than customer satisfaction ratings, for example) was available and was consulted during the problem definition phase.
- The missing *knowledge and skills*, those which would be needed to execute the strategy successfully, were correctly identified.

THE HUMAN PERFORMANCE IMPROVEMENT MODEL AT NOVELL

In its application to customer support excellence at Novell, the HPI model unites an amazing variety of activity, which requires a good deal of energy. But when energy is focused by this model, it supplies a great deal of energy, and change happens.

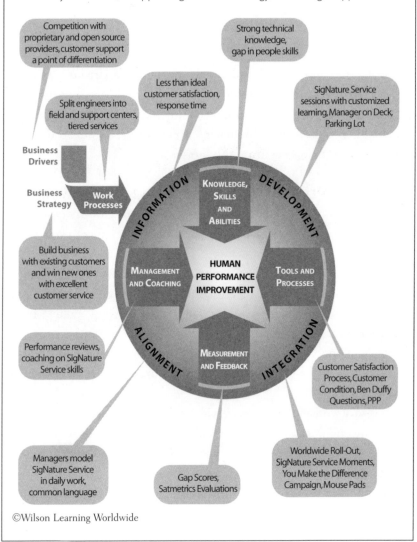

©Wilson Learning Worldwide

- The *development* or classroom-training phase was customized to Novell's needs and goals and made directly applicable to engineers' and managers' daily work.
- The *tools and processes* had immediate impact, and both reinforcement and performance measures were tied to them to ensure long-term assimilation.
- *Measurement and feedback*, both from customer evaluations and management's coaching, continued to foster ongoing improvement.
- As a result of all these things, but also as a goal that was accomplished, Novell's customer support unit is fully *aligned* in this change, even down to its corporate communications.
- Managers and executives made it a highly visible priority to participate themselves and coached their teams in ways that insured they embraced the change as a way of working.

The success of this implementation not only gives Novell the best possible customer support it can deliver, but it also opens the door for broader corporate success. And it makes the people involved in this strategy feel good about their work. Customer support may well be "the toughest job in business," but when both the customer and the support person come away feeling really satisfied, there's a good chance they'll both come back for more.

INDEX

Adapting toward the customer, 76

Alignment, 14, 16, 36-37

Ask for an expression
of satisfaction, 65, 99

Ben Duffy, 51, 59, 70-72, 81, 96

Bicycle model, 59-60

Bench, Cory, 7, 47

Bunch, Marion, 7, 32-34, 37-39,
83, 95

Business development, 23, 43

Business drivers, 11, 14, 105

Business processes, 14-15, 20

Business strategy, 14, 22

Classroom, 39, 43, 46, 50-54,
57, 59, 71, 81, 83, 93-94, 107

Coach, 12, 16, 35, 51, 52, 81-82

Coaching, 7, 53, 57, 82, 93, 107

Comfortable customer, 66-68,
77, 79, 89, 98-99

Competence, 59

Conclude, 65, 78-79, 94, 99

Cordes, Marc, 7, 91-92

Credibility, 23, 32, 52, 57, 70-71

Cultural differences, 91

Culture, 26, 32, 38, 87-89

Customer condition, 66-69, 79,
83, 92-93, 98

Customer Satisfaction Approach,
58, 65, 79, 83

Customize, 12, 27, 31, 34, 38,
81, 107

Cutler, Dave, 7, 24-26, 31-34,
36, 44, 87, 92, 96, 100-101

De Koning, Gemma, 7, 48, 89

Define the problem, 13-14, 31

Development, 13-15, 19-20, 33,
37, 51, 107

Discovery, 33-35, 38, 73, 81, 96

Discovery agreement, 73-75, 83

Dissatisfaction, 61-62

Dissatisfied customer, 61-63, 80

Diversity, 39, 88-90

Emotional condition, 7, 32, 58,
66, 79, 89, 92-93

Empathy, 23, 57, 59-60, 70, 75,
98

Expectation, 25, 49, 58, 62, 65,
72, 77, 79, 87, 90-91, 99

Explanations, 73-74

Expression of satisfaction, 65, 76,
99, 102

Fear, 37, 39, 62-64, 66, 69, 73
Flexibility, 59-60, 99
Follow the sun support, 24, 87
Fulfillment, 7, 11-12
Gap, 14, 34, 96
Gap Analysis, 33-34, 95
Gap score, 100-102
Global expansion, 87
Gomez, Rodrigo, 7, 92
Haug, Barry, 7, 24, 28, 32-33, 35, 49
HELPR tool, 53, 82
HPI, see Human Performance Improvement
Hudson, Noel, 34, 37
Human Performance Improvement (HPI), 12-16, 16, 19, 35-36, 50, 105-106
Indecisive customer, 66, 69, 79, 89, 99
Information, 14-15
Insistent customer, 66, 69, 79, 89, 99
Integrating, 16, 87
Integration, 14-16, 83, 87
Interact, 65, 98-99
Irate customer, 66, 68, 79, 89, 93, 99
Jensen, Lorin, 95
Leader, 12-15, 25, 43, 105
Leadership, 4, 11, 16, 38
Lowry, Bruce, 7
Lyons, Mike, 8, 23, 25-26, 28, 33
Management, 12, 14, 20-21, 27, 35-38, 44, 46-47, 49, 51, 57, 97, 107

Manager, 7, 14, 16, 23-24, 32, 36-37, 43-44, 49-53, 57, 71-72, 81, 83-84, 89-91, 93-96, 107
Manager on Deck, 47-53, 58, 82
Measure, 14, 16, 31, 36-37, 52, 87, 97-98, 100-101, 107
Measurement gap, 15
Model, 7, 35, 37, 48, 52, 57, 59, 83-84, 93
Needs, 12, 16, 21, 25-28, 58, 60, 65, 67, 69, 71-72, 74, 76-79, 81, 83, 87-88, 97
Novell Technical Service (NTS), 11, 23, 44
Objective, 61
Open, 11, 20-21, 23, 38, 47, 51, 65-66, 71, 78-79, 90, 96, 105
Palme, Carl, 8, 88-89, 95, 101-102
Palmer, Brad, 8, 44-46, 49, 50-51, 53, 64, 81-82, 93-94, 100, 102
Parking Lot, 47-49, 52-53, 88
Paxton, Derek, 8, 45, 71, 75, 83, 93, 101
Performance, 15-16, 25, 31, 35, 37, 43, 61, 64, 87, 93-96, 99-100
Performance gap, 15
Performance measure, 13, 96-97, 100, 105, 107
Personalizing, 67-68, 99
Purpose, 46, 52, 61, 71, 82
Purpose, Process, Payoff (PPP), 71-72, 74, 81, 93

Rapport, 65-67, 70, 78-79
Recovery skills, 79-80
Refresher courses, 48, 88, 95
Reinforce, 14, 35, 46, 57, 59, 66, 70-71, 74, 77, 81, 87, 92-93, 95, 107
Reinforcement tools, 82
Reward, 16, 39, 48, 52
Riddell, Tevilla, 8, 34-37, 39, 44, 46, 48-49, 50, 71, 82-83, 88-89
Satisfaction, 7, 23, 35-37, 39-40, 49, 57-59, 61-63, 65, 67, 77, 79-80, 84, 94, 97-102, 105
Saying no, 74, 99
Self-management, 60, 63-65, 80
Self-talk, 52, 63-64, 75, 79-80
Skill, 7, 12-15, 23-24, 32-37, 39-40, 43-46, 49, 51-53, 58-60, 65, 72, 75-76, 81-84, 87-89, 93-98, 100, 105
Skill development, 15
Skill gap, 15
Skill training, 35, 43-44, 87, 94
Stop-Challenge-Focus, 64, 66, 80
Strategy, 11-16, 21-23, 25, 36, 43, 50-51, 58, 84, 87, 95-96, 101, 105, 107
Sumsion, Jim, 8, 59, 83, 93
Support skill, 34, 36-37, 40, 43-44, 89, 94, 105
Support skill training, 43-44, 87, 94
Sustainable change, 7, 13-14, 24, 93, 105
Szechy, Akos, 8, 92

Technical know-how, 11, 39, 76, 94
Technical knowledge, 32, 73, 84
Technical skills, 23, 32, 59, 105
Tool, 7, 12-15, 27, 32-33, 35-36, 38, 74, 83-84, 90, 94, 96-98, 100, 107
Tool gap, 15
Training, 13, 15, 27, 31, 33, 35-36, 39, 43-54, 57, 59, 63, 74, 81-83, 87, 89, 92-96, 100-102, 107
Transformation, 7, 13, 16, 19, 25, 31, 36, 43, 92, 97
Trust, 23, 38-39, 45, 57, 67, 70, 81, 92
Validation, 66, 68, 79
Value, 11-12, 23, 33, 35, 37, 49, 88
Vendor, 20, 28, 31-32, 34-35, 38, 43, 100
Wilson Learning, 4, 7, 12, 14-16, 32-35, 37-38, 59, 61, 70, 88, 95-96
Work process gaps, 15
You Make the Difference campaign, 46, 52, 82, 94
Zone of Indifference, 61-62
Zotkin, Igor, 8, 91, 95, 101-102

ABOUT THE AUTHORS

Nova Vista Publishing's Best Practices Editors are a group of executives, managers, consultants and business writers who team up from time to time to examine remarkable business transformation stories in human terms, using real business cases. The team assembled for this book includes the following people:

Marion Bunch, Partner, Strategy Implementation Resource

Dave Cutler, Vice President, Novell Support Services, Novell, Inc.

Kathe Grooms, Managing Director, Nova Vista Publishing

Barry Haug, Director, Novell Mid-West Area, Novell, Inc.

Andrew Karre, Editor

Michael Leimbach, Vice President, Research and Design,
Wilson Learning Americas

Bruce Lowry, Director of Public Relations, Novell, Inc.

Michael Lyons, Vice President, Novell Global Support Services,
Novell, Inc.

Brad Palmer, Manager, Novell Support Services, Novell Inc.

Tevilla Riddell, Principal, The Riddell Resources

David Yesford, Vice President, Worldwide Solutions Management,
Wilson Learning Americas